Standing as Awareness

Standing as Awareness

The Direct Path

GREG GOODE

Foreword by Jerry Katz

NON-DUALITY PRESS

STANDING AS AWARENESS
Revised edition
First published September 2009 by NON-DUALITY PRESS

© Greg Goode 2009
© Non-Duality Press 2009
Cover design by John Gustard

Typeset in Guardi 10.5/15 & Stone Sans

Non-Duality Press | PO Box 2228 | Salisbury | SP2 2GZ
United Kingdom

ISBN: 978-0-9563091-5-0

www.non-dualitypress.com

Contents

Acknowledgements

I'd like to thank Dr. Tomas Sander, scientist, student of happiness and joyful irony, for his sharp-eyed editorial assistance. Michael Rosker was at the very first Nondual Dinner gatherings back in 1997, and his enthusiasm, insatiable curiosity and good cheer helped keep the gatherings going through the early years – sometimes weekly, sometimes monthly. Daniel Singer, co-author of *The Sacred Portable Now*, has helped organize the gatherings in the last five years. His personality is graced with an engaging combination of rare wisdom, great compassion, natural irony, and a down-to-earth sense of humor. A special thanks goes out to Julian Noyce of Non-Duality Press for encouraging me to republish this.

Foreword
by Jerry Katz

I first met Greg Goode when I started Nonduality.com and the Nonduality Salon discussion e-group in 1998. Everyone liked Greg, including the most intellectually unforgiving and the most enlightened.

Greg's an ordinary guy who treats everyone the same. He can speak of Richard Rorty's nondual philosophy and riding a bike with the same enthusiasm and affection.

I've met Greg at retreats a couple of times. I love how he explodes into laughter at something you said which you didn't think was so funny. Makes you wonder what he was really laughing at.

And I've seen tears roll down his eyes when talking to a group of people about the sweetness of awareness.

Ten years since we first met on the Internet, we were still involved with each other. When I was asked to co-organize the Science and Nonduality Conference for October, 2009, its scope required a partner. The first person I thought of was Greg Goode. He was invaluable in that role, bringing organization, understanding of what we were trying to accomplish, and knowledge of who's who. He was easy as pie to work with.

Describing "standing as awareness" as "free, light, weightless, uncrowded, unburdened, sweet and peacefully present," Greg describes himself.

If you want to become enlightened, you will be thankful for the direct path teaching as set forth here.

Greg starts this book with the bold and direct invitation to take your stand as awareness. From there Greg raises and hones in on questions you may not even known you have, all the while conversational about it:

"How does one take a stand as awareness?"

"What about pain?"

"I would like to have the same kind of enlightenment experience I read about others having."

"At satsangs I've gotten very close to enlightenment, but then it seemed to go away."

"Can you be attached to awareness?"

"Which teachings are true?"

Key to this book are simple experiments whose purpose is to expose experience as awareness. To do these experiments you need everyday objects in front of you, such as a table, cups, and your own body and senses.

Greg leads you from the experiential to deeper inquiry into what you consider yourself to be.

What's powerful and new about this book is the degree of subtlety and discernment regarding seekers, teachers, satsang, inquiry, language.

Earlier I mentioned that Greg talks with passion about riding a bike. He rides a track bike. It's ridden by racers and the best zen-like couriers. A track bike has no brakes.

The teaching here does not stop short, does not leave the smallest separation between experience and awareness. In your hands you hold a book with no brakes. You are invited to turn the page and begin pedaling.

Jerry Katz
Nonduality.com
Editor, *One: Essential Writings on Nonduality*

Preface

The book's title was chosen in recognition of one of the teachings from Sri Atmananda (Krishna Menon, 1883–1959), author of *Atma Darshan* and *Atma Nivriti*. By standing as awareness, you experience the world as awareness quite directly, without having to perfect anything or become anything.

This is a revised edition of the book, expanded from the edition that was published as an e-book in 2007. That edition was a book of dialogs from dinner conversations that took place between 1997 and 2005 in New York City at what are called "Nondual Dinners." These gatherings, still taking place about once a month, were originally inspired by Francis Lucille when he began coming to New York City. He encouraged people to get together in friendship, love and openness as he (and before him Jean Klein) had done in Europe decades previously.

Francis and Jean, like myself, have been deeply influenced by Sri Atmananda's teaching. It is known as the "direct path," which happens to be the same term that Ramana Maharshi applied to his teaching. In both cases, "direct" means "not progressive." There is no need to progress closer and closer to the desired spiritual goal. One has always been at home there.

In the years since the book's initial publication, I received many comments and requests that boiled down to two issues. People wanted a more step-by-step unfolding of the teaching, and they wanted exercises, experiments or guided meditations.

Towards that end, I added three chapters. They cover the fundamentals of the direct path, such as how to take your stand as awareness, what happens when you fall in love with awareness, and how to conduct your exploration of awareness. The steps take you from the initial interest in the subject all the way to the peaceful collapse of the witness into pure consciousness. I also added several experiments in which you investigate various dualistic aspects of experience, and discover that your experience is simply undivided nondual awareness all along.

The presentation you are about to read could be shorter. And it could be longer. This one is the medium-size version!

How to Stand as Awareness

What is awareness anyway?

Before talking about standing as awareness, let's talk about awareness itself. Awareness sees what arises. Whatever appears, appears to awareness. In order for form, thought, feeling, sensation, time, space, unity and multiplicity to appear to awareness, awareness itself cannot be limited or defined by these factors. Awareness is the single subject of all objects. It is the formless that sees all form. It is the unseen seer.

Sometimes awareness is called consciousness. The two terms are synonymous in this teaching. Sometimes awareness is called being. This is to underscore that awareness is not nonexistence or voidness. Sometimes it is called knowledge. This is to convey that it is the antidote to ignorance. And sometimes awareness is called love. This is to emphasize its open, inviting, generous, intimate nature that is free from limitation and suffering.

You can experience your being as awareness easily. Whereas the teachings say that awareness is the seer of all that is seen, you experience seeing directly as happening in you. You never directly experience seeing to happen anywhere else. You don't even "see" seeing. It is much closer than that. It always feels as though it is happening *here*. It always feels like "I" am what is seeing.

Awareness sees, and I see. They are the same thing. Awareness *is* the "I", or as Sri Atmananda calls it, the "I-principle."

Awareness is not an object

This leads to a realization that seems trivial now but will have transformational consequences later: since awareness or the I-principle is that which sees (since it is the subject of seeing), awareness itself cannot be seen. Awareness is not an object, but the subject. It is not the thing seen, but rather that which sees.

The reason that this will prove to be transformational is that will dissolve the seeking tendency that tries to objectify or behold awareness. If you hear that awareness is your nature, it then becomes quite natural for you to want to bring awareness up close and personal. You wish to zoom in on it before your mind's eye, or to behold it in front of you as though it were sitting on a plate.

But awareness does not occur as an object. Sure, you can think of *concepts* of awareness, utter *terms* supposedly representative of awareness, or see artistic *renderings* of awareness. But notice that in each case, what is directly experienced is a concept, a word or a picture. Awareness itself hasn't been captured. After all, even if you think about this in an everyday logical way outside the scope of nondual teachings, it makes sense: for there to be all these objects, there must be some subject for them to appear to. Why should the subject itself be able to be an object as well?

And then, if you think about this more deeply, it will make more sense – to examine something mentally or visually is what is done with *objects*; it can't be done to that which *sees objects*. You can't catch this seeing in the act. You can experience this inability at any time. Just try to see awareness itself, or perhaps do the Douglas Harding experiments. Each time, you will fail spectacularly!

The more this difference between objects and awareness sinks in, the less one tries to prove awareness through looking at something special. One no longer tries to keep awareness close, or grasp onto certain objects that are believed to be definitive of awareness. There is great liberation in this!

Awareness is always already there. It is infinitely closer than any concept, term or image. It is that open clarity within which these objects arise. It is that in which they subsist, and that into which they subside. It is present even when they are not. It is the open, loving spaciousness of YOU.

Quick tour of standing as awareness

What if you took a stand, right now, as awareness? Sure, it can seem that "everything is awareness" is almost a cliché these days. But what if you really treated this pronouncement, this recent cliché, as true? Simply, you will discover that experience confirms your stand.

At the beginning of one's search, it certainly doesn't seem this way. It seems that experience is a very dualistic affair. Experience, we are taught early in life, has a personal inner observer who gets in touch with outer objects through the means of the senses, and communicates through language to other inner observers. There is an impassible barrier, we are taught, between *in* and *out*.

Many years of this cultural conditioning makes this inner-observer model feel so convincing that it is rarely questioned. This way of experiencing corresponds to a stand taken as the gross body. You feel as if you're the observer beholding a world outside. As intimately related to a physical object (i.e., the gross body), you naturally experience the world as a large collection of physical objects.

If you stand as awareness, however, the world will be experienced as awareness itself. Experience will no longer be felt as a dualistic affair. It won't seem as though experience is of anything or centralized anywhere. "Experience," as a word used by teachers of the direct path, is a synonym for awareness itself.

How your stand determines your experience

Experience usually seems dualistic, divided into an experiencer (subject) and that which is experienced (the object). This subject/object duality is perhaps the most fundamental duality of all. The two sides are related to each other. How you see yourself affects how you see the object of your experience. "What you be" determines what you see. And vice versa.

And yet not all of your experience seems split up into this dualism. There are many times such as being "in the zone," caught up in a beautiful sunset or exciting movie, or being in deep sleep, when there is no subject/object gap felt whatsoever. At these times you stand as the zone, or the flow or the sunset or movie itself, which is another way of saying that you were standing as awareness.

Throughout the day, throughout life, you stand as different things. This "standing" isn't necessarily something you do or necessarily the outcome of a decision or commit-ment. "Standing" characterizes the relationship between you and what you experience.

When you stand as body, you experience bodies

This is when it seems that your "I" is the body itself or in the material body. What you experience seems to be a world of other material bodies, both inert and alive.

When you stand as mind, you experience minds

This is when it seems that your "I" is the mind or in the mind. What you experience seems to be a world of other minds and flowing energies making up the phenomenal world. Even those times when you look back at one of those timeless and gapless moments and say that it was "really" a psychological quirk – saying that, you are standing as mind.

When you stand as awareness, awareness is your experience

This is when either (a) the objects you witness don't seem like bodies, minds, particles, relations or any kind of entity at all, but merely appearances in awareness. They don't signify or refer to anything outside of experience, or inside experience either, for that matter. This is the higher witness. Or (b) when you don't experience objects or appearances at all, but rather awareness or consciousness is self-luminously shining. This is when the witness has dissolved or collapsed into pure consciousness.

How do you do it?

You can start by acknowledging that during a given 24-hour period, you stand as awareness much of the time already, such as during those moments mentioned earlier when there is no experienced subject/object gap. These times account for much more of the day than you might think, especially if you include deep sleep.

Even during the other times, when it seems that you experience a world of physical and mental objects, you can take some time to notice the parallels between "I" and awareness. These are the parallels between (a) that which experiences, and (b) consciousness. The self that experiences doesn't perceive consciousness, and consciousness doesn't perceive the self. Neither has shape, color or location. Both are directly experienced as subjects, not objects. They are the same thing, and are what all objects appear to.

So the "I" JUST IS awareness. Sri Atmananda calls the self "the I-principle." Taking advantage of this insight, you can take your stand as follows. "OK then, so what goes for awareness goes for me." What follows from this, when deeply seen, will transform your experience.

- Awareness doesn't suffer; neither do I.
- Awareness doesn't come and go; neither do I.
- Awareness is open and spacious; so am I.
- There are no limits, edges or borders to awareness; none to me either.
- Awareness is present during the presence of objects, during the absence of objects and beyond all objects; so am I.

Based on these insights, your experience will begin to verify the stand you have taken. Asserting your stand is like claiming your birthright. It is like coming home after a journey.

You acknowledge, "I am home – as awareness. We are the same thing!" It needn't seem presumptuous, since you can't be wrong about it.

Experiment with being awareness

> To get a taste of being awareness, here's something you can do at any time during the day or night. Take a moment and just be, without preconceived notions, even notions about awareness. Don't be a body or mind. Don't take yourself as anything at all. And just openly notice how images and appearances and even gestalts and points of view come and go. Check to see whether you have the experience that YOU come and go. Or do you as witnessing awareness remain perfectly and peacefully present and unmoving, clear and open?

Confirmation

Taking a stand as awareness is not cheating. It is not a case of spiritual bypassing or claiming something you haven't earned. It is more like stepping into the living room of your own home. And there are many pointers that confirm the stand you take as awareness. And if you happen to fall in love with awareness, you will find even more confirmation.

Amazingly, one confirmation comes through language! This is amazing because language is often thought to be a barrier or a block to an experience of the truth. But when you stand as awareness, language actually becomes transformed into a confirmation of your stand.

For example, you come to see that all words point to awareness. Nouns refer not to things, but directly to awareness because (a) awareness is the nature of all things, and (b) awareness is the only thing actually touched, or pointed to or referred to by words. It is all that is available to refer to – you simply can't find any other referents. Verbs express awareness, one might say, by "I-ing." Pronouns also point directly to awareness. "You," "I," "she," "he," "we," and "they" also point directly there in the same way that nouns do.

When you say "I," it emerges from awareness and also refers back to awareness, which is how it truly refers. Even the very thought "I" points to awareness by vanishing as thoughts do into awareness. This I is not personal. It is not your I or Greg's I. No one can have a separate I since there is no way to divide awareness.

You come to see that no one has a more direct relationship to "I" than anyone else. Rather, you and others and everything are all this I-principle, which is awareness itself. Bodies and borders and divisions that you'd normally think separate one thing from another are all this selfsame awareness, which is nothing other than I. Even the seemingly painful events of stubbing your toe or going to the dentist are nothing other than pure experience, awareness, the I-principle. These events are all empty of truly being anything else.

This is the nature of direct experience. Free, unbordered, undivided and peaceful. Everything is just like this.

Falling in Love with Awareness

Many people never hear about this "stand as awareness" teaching. But many who encounter nondual teachings actually fall in love with awareness, which is another way of occupying one's stand. One's love for awareness is always answered; it is never an unrequited love. The way awareness answers this call of love establishes you and the world as awareness. Here are some signs of falling in love with awareness:

- You yearn to immerse yourself fully in awareness
- You feel more interested in awareness than the objects that appear to awareness
- You yearn for a clearer understanding of awareness
- You feel you understand it intellectually, but that there must be more
- You get a sense of a sweetness that comes directly from awareness, and an intuition that there's more...
- You wonder why the sweetness comes and goes
- You deeply wonder, "If awareness is the sum and substance of everything, why does it seem as though there are things other than awareness?"

Falling in love with awareness consists of being pulled by the curiosity, the yearning, the sweetness. This love is always answered fully by awareness itself. The answer is an opening into a broader, more global experience of awareness, as awareness. The curiosity and yearning are satisfied, the sweetness spreads, and you come to experience as awareness things that previously seemed to be other than awareness. The sweetness spreads until you come to experience yourself and the world as one undivided awareness.

When you fall in love with awareness, you desire to draw near. The direct-path teachings emphasize an investigative, exploratory way of drawing near to awareness. Because even after hearing the teachings, many people feel that there is a near and far, or a difference between awareness and something other than awareness.

Drawn by one's love of awareness, one investigates this presumed difference. The investigation is like a treasure hunt, where the clues consist of the sweetness you intuit as you draw near. Finding the treasure is finding that there is no difference, that there is nothing other than awareness.

Higher reason

Sri Atmananda and other direct-path teachers mention "higher reason" as the way you go about your exploration.

It's called "higher reason" so as to distinguish it from everyday reason, which is a calculative process. Higher reason is empowered by your love of awareness and is not calculative, but more holistic. It is as though you stand "above the mind" as awareness, which allows you to investigate the nature of the mind and its machinery.

In a nutshell, higher reason works by following your

direct experience. You examine the gross and subtle worlds, as well as the body, senses and mind. You come to see that they are experienced as objects in witnessing awareness and cannot exist apart from witnessing awareness. You then investigate the witness itself and come to see that it is an ever-so-subtle structure superimposed upon awareness. When this is realized, the witness gently and peacefully collapses into awareness itself, which is pure consciousness. Higher reason establishes that pure consciousness is the truth of the world and your experience at every moment, and leaves you unshakably established in this truth.

Higher reason follows the canons of scientific investigation. It adheres to empirical evidence, and it can be replicated by you and others. It is roughly equivalent to jnana yoga as mentioned in traditional Advaita Vedanta. Jnana yoga is described as coming to know the transitory versus the permanent or the "field" versus the "knower of the field" (*Bhagavad Gita*, chapter 13). In terms of the direct path, higher reason investigates the difference between the objects that arise to awareness, and awareness itself. It shows that there is no difference.

Even for those who don't really feel in *love* with awareness, there are still pragmatic reasons to engage in this investigation. Basically, this investigation provides a subtle, powerful and time-tested set of tools to dissolve one's sense of separation and alienation.

How do you begin?

The best way to begin is with the most tangible aspect of experience. You begin with what seems most obviously *different* from awareness – the physical world. The physical world seems hard, solid, heavy, impenetrable, independent and pre-existent. It seems like it's really there! We feel pushed about by it. But awareness seems vast, open, giving, soft and embracing. How can physical objects like the Empire State Building and the Brooklyn Bridge actually be ... awareness?

Higher reason proceeds like this. It shows that the external object cannot be separated from sensory form. Then, you come to see that form cannot be separated from seeing because the idea of seeing goes into the very makeup of form. Next you realize that seeing cannot be separated from awareness. To see is to be aware. To not see is also to be aware. Throughout all your experience of the objective world, awareness is the only constant and present factor.

Awareness is open, clear and loving. It embraces everything, and refuses nothing. It is present even when the physical world is not given in experience, such as in dreams or deep sleep. So when you begin your investigation, you start with your direct experience, which is awareness. You actually have no other place to begin. As you investigate the difference between awareness and what seems to be other than awareness, you open and embrace this "other" and discover that it is actually your self. Let's try some higher reason.

Experiment with a cup

Let's start with a tiny piece of the physical world – a teacup!

If you can, go get a teacup or a coffee cup and put it on an uncluttered area of the table or desk in front of you.

Sit down with your hands in your lap. Look at the

cup with a soft, open focus. Notice that there may be thoughts arising, perhaps thoughts about where the cup came from, what it is made out of, etc. Notice that these thoughts could still arise even if your eyes were closed, so they are not part of your direct experience of the cup. Let these thoughts pass by and attend only to the direct visual experience of the cup.

What is directly given in your visual experience of the cup? What does vision experience? There are color and shape, which together are often called "form." Notice that you don't experience color without shape, or shape without color. Notice that what you take to be the shape of the cup is actually based on the interface between two shades of color. Looking to the edges of the cup, you can notice that where the cup ends and where the table around it begins is actually based on where one color comes to an end and another color begins.

Following your direct visual experience, you can notice that various "objective" characteristics you normally attribute to a cup are here based on color. This includes "distance," "size," "weight," "height," "depth," "roundness," "texture," "smoothness," and "hardness" are based on nothing other than regions and interfaces of color. Now, try to find the various aspects of color that stand for these supposedly objective characteristics. For example, notice that you don't see distance or weight, but they are based on associations and conclusions made from various colors. For example, consider depth: no color is experienced to be in front or in back of another color. Instead, *unbroken* regions of color suggest "in front of"; *broken* or *interrupted* regions of color suggest "in back of," etc. Try to experience how color suggests the other qualities.

What is realized in this experiment?

You realize this – through a series of stages, the cup you had earlier thought to be an independent physical object is actually nothing other than awareness itself. The stages can be seen as follows:

1. The cup is not separate from form. Visually, you experience colors and form. But vision does not directly pick up anything beyond that. It can be transformational and perhaps thrilling to realize how much actually does *not* appear to direct visual experience. You do not directly experience any independence of the cup. In other words, vision itself does not communicate anything like "cup that exists whether you see it or not." In fact you do not directly experience independence or separation at all.

You do not actually experience a *cup* apart from the forms (colors and shapes) that are your direct experience at this moment. You do not experience these colors and shapes pointing outside of themselves to a true, physical cup lying beyond. You have no way of getting between these visual forms and a "real" cup so as to be able to compare the colors to the cup. None of that is given in your direct experience. The colors and shapes directly given in vision do not communicate that it they are "about" the cup or that they "refer to" the cup or that they are "caused by" the cup. *Aboutness, reference* and *causation* are not part of your direct experience. Sure, there are intellectual theories about these abstract things, but they are not seen or given in your direct visual experience. So there is no cup given in direct experience.

2. Form is not separate from seeing. Next, you come to realize that you do not experience *form* apart from the faculty of *seeing*. You cannot separate form from seeing, even in imagination. You cannot get between seeing and form in order to make a comparison. You have no experience of pre-existing forms, some which happen to be seen, and some which happen not to be seen. An unseen form is not experienced anywhere, just like an unthought thought.

This leads to the shocking realization that you do not see form at any time! Form is not something external that is independent of seeing; form goes into the very idea of seeing. Seeing is not a function that *operates* on form, it is another word *for* form. So you do not actually see form.

3. Seeing is not separate from witnessing awareness. Next, you come to realize that seeing itself cannot be separated from the awareness to which it arises. When seeing is present, its presence is noted by awareness. When seeing is absent, its absence is noted by awareness. Other than awareness, seeing has no other independent way of arising or being experienced. You have no other access to seeing. You cannot get between awareness and seeing to watch them make contact with each other. When seeing is not present, it is not like an actor in the wings, waiting to come onstage.

This leads to another fresh realization – because seeing is not something that happens independently of awareness, you are actually not ever aware *of* seeing. It makes no sense to think that seeing is truly an object. Rather, awareness is actually another word *for* seeing. Because seeing has nowhere to go and nothing to be other than awareness, awareness is actually the nature of seeing. This same nature cascades

15

all the way through to the supposed physical object, which itself is nothing other than awareness. This is your direct experience at all times.

The other senses are the same as seeing

What goes for seeing also applies to hearing, smelling, tasting and touching. Keeping to the direct evidence of the particular sense itself, you realize that the sense object cannot be separated from the sense modality. The sense modality cannot be separated from witnessing awareness. Witnessing awareness is present through all experiences "of" the supposed physical world, and nothing is experienced independently or apart from this awareness.

The sense of touch sometimes seems to be an exception. For those who feel that the physical world is the benchmark of reality, nothing feels more "real" than hitting your thumb with a hammer, or knocking your knee on the computer under your desk. To many people, pain is thought to be more real than most other experiences. Yet upon investigation, it can be seen that pain is not something we would attribute to objects in the physical world. Pain is an arising experience and simply cannot prove the reality of an object. It is the same for the rest of our direct experience through the sense of touch.

If you repeat the cup experiment using the sense of touch, you can realize same series of stages you realized earlier. If you close your eyes, and attend only to the direct experience given through touching, you'll see that what arises is a series of sensations of texture, warmth or coolness, and hardness. These sensations arise, then fall. You can come to realize the following: (1) There is no cup experienced separate from the sensations. The sensations themselves simply don't communicate an object independent of the sensations. (2) Furthermore, these sensations are not separate from the faculty of touch. One doesn't touch any pre-existing sensations; touch is another word for these sensations. (3) Touch isn't separate from witnessing awareness. Touch never arises in the absence of witnessing awareness. As they say about turtles, it's awareness all the way down!

The body is awareness

The direct path is one of the few nondual approaches that investigate the body directly. The body normally falls under the category of "physical object," but it seems like a very special physical object. Unlike other objects, it seems to accompany you wherever you go. And if you tap it, say, with a pencil or pen, certain sensations arise that never arise if you tap the cup or the table. And most importantly, it seems as though the body is the container of awareness, of *your* awareness. *Your* awareness seems different from the awareness of others. What seems to separate them is often thought to be the walls of the body. Your body seems to contain your awareness, and other bodies seem to contain other awarenesses. But with the help of higher reason, you can come to recognize the body as arisings in awareness. As arisings in awareness, the body can't enclose awareness. It can be nothing other than awareness. This liberates and globalizes your understanding of awareness, which will no longer seem bottled up in the body. As awareness itself, the body is free and no longer seems to compartmentalize awareness.

Let's try another experiment in higher reason.

Experiment with your arm

Let's take a look at just one part of the body, your arm and see if it lets itself be experienced as awareness...

Lay your arm on the table in front of you.

The direct visual experience of your arm is parallel to what you experienced with the cup. There are colors and shapes given to visual experience. Even if the arm moves, movement is just experienced visually as changes in color and shape. There is no visual experience of an arm apart from form, no experience of form apart from seeing, and no experience of seeing apart from awareness.

Now close your eyes so as to focus on touch. If you touch your arm, your experience is parallel to what you experienced with the cup. Even though there seem to be two sources of sensation (the touching hand and the touched arm), this is based on the assumption that sources are external physical objects. But these same feelings could appear in dreams as well. The very notion of "source" or "location" is merely an intellectual conclusion arising after the fact of your direct experience. The direct experience of touch doesn't communicate source or location, but has its own language as vision did. Touch communicates the sensations of texture, warmth, softness or hardness, maybe ticklishness, pleasantness or unpleasantness.

Keeping your eyes shut, move your arm above the table about a foot, then slowly left and right, and then back down, you will feel a slightly different type of sensation. This is often called kinesthesis or somesthesis. This is the sense of what we call positionality or movement. This sense appears and disappears, and like all the other components of our direct experience that we have examined, this sense never establishes an object independent of the sensations themselves.

With your eyes closed, repeat the movement and examine the sensations openly and directly, without history, memory or theory. Following your direct experience, try to find an independently existing physical object that is undergoing the movement. Direct experience will not provide such an object. You'll be able to realize the same shocking things as before – that experience establishes no object apart from the sensations, no sensations apart from the feeling sense, and no feeling sense apart from witnessing awareness. Again, it is witnessing awareness that is the only element constantly present throughout.

Objection – "But this *can't* be true!'

Quite often it's about at this point that the mind kicks in and says, "But wait a minute!" Even though we can't really argue with the authority of direct experience, it can start to seem outlandish that physical objects including the body simply don't exist independently of awareness. The most common objection is that without independently existing physical objects, we would never be able to explain experience. It seems that we could never even eat dinner without objects. It seems that the world simply cannot make sense unless object exist to cause experience.

This can be a very strong feeling, and it's based on centuries of conditioning.[1] There are many ways to address this objection, but there are two that relate to the direct experience yielded by higher reason.

One response is this – even if we concede that there must be external objects to serve as the cause and explanation of our experience, we'd be back at the exact same point anyway. This is because in spite of our concession, the only evidence we have for these objects (and any causal chain issuing from them) boils down to the very same direct experience we already examined in our experiments. Awareness is still established as the sum and substance of our experience. Verbally or intellectually granting independence to objects does not make them more evident. Either way, we're back with awareness as all that is truly established by direct experience.

---

1. Serious philosophizing about this kind of thinking began in the seventeenth century with philosophers such as René Descartes and John Locke, as well as with scientists who modeled human knowledge upon the theory of optics from Johannes Kepler. These thinkers became extremely influential in Western culture; they conceived of the person as having an internal point of sentience encased in a body. Humankind's essence was to accurately represent an outside world in thought, and communicate it to others. Before that era, experience and knowledge were thought to be much more organic and holistic, without imposing metaphysical barriers between internal and external. For two extremely lucid deconstructions of this spectator view of human knowledge, see Colin M. Turbayne's *The Myth of Metaphor* (New Haven, Connecticut: Yale Univ. Press, 1962) and Richard Rorty's *Philosophy and the Mirror of Nature* (Princeton, New Jersey: Princeton University Press, 1979).

The other response is pragmatic. Just because direct experience establishes that the gross world is nothing but awareness doesn't force us to speak in any particular way. We don't have to talk Advaita-talk at the grocery store. There's no reason we must abandon the conventional vocabularies used in science, mechanics, architecture and other disciplines. These arenas of human activity posit for their own local purposes objects that exist independently of the means of measurement. Let's say you're working in a profession with such a dominant physicalist view. You can still participate without having to believe the view, refute it, or argue with your supervisors! You can look at the view as a kind of ornate modern poetry. The implicit view can be used just fine without being believed. You can also look at vocabularies as themselves arisings in awareness. You are free to allow a vocabulary to arise in its own natural way.

The mind is an object, not the subject

So far, our investigation has revealed that the physical world and the body are actually awareness, even though they originally seemed to be quite other than awareness. Continuing with our investigation, we examine the mind as another candidate for something that seems to be other than awareness.

The mind seems to be other than awareness in several ways. For example, it may seem to be the place where awareness happens. Or it might seem that
- the mind contains awareness the way a jack o'lantern contains the light from a candle
- the mind is the location of awareness
- the mind can perceive awareness

- the mind can direct or control awareness
- awareness flows through the mind the way electricity flows through wires
- awareness is inscribed in the mind as software is installed on a hard drive

These are all ways that one can tend to think about awareness and the mind. Some of these analogies are taught in spiritual teachings. Notice that all these analogies are based on physical metaphors such as containment or visual perception, and that these metaphors condition your thinking in terms of inside and outside. We have already seen that the physical can be nothing separate from awareness. The same goes for the mind.

We can see this because our direct experience is quite the opposite from what these analogies and metaphors suggest. In direct experience, awareness is not located in the mind, but the mind arises as an object in awareness. Even in everyday terms, you have noticed when the mind is calm and peaceful, and when the mind is agitated and jumpy. But you never experience the mind playing host to awareness, enclosing awareness, or controlling awareness like the Panama Canal controls the flow of water. And if you pursue this inquiry and look even closer for the mind, you don't find any container at all, but just a stream of thoughts. You find thoughts, but never a *holder* of thoughts.

And since thoughts cannot possibly exist outside of awareness, awareness is the only thing for them to be made of. This last statement is a bit indirect, but it will become crystal clear later when all objects are directly experienced as dissolving into pure consciousness.

The Witness – from Establishment to Collapse

When objects arise, they never come self-identified as "thought" vs. "feeling" vs. "sensation." Even if the "thought" is labeled by another thought, the two actually never cross paths, as you will see in the experiment below. So there is no reason to conclude that what arises is *really* a thought, feeling or sensation. These terms were helpful earlier on when we used them to realize that physical and mental structures are not real objects independent of awareness. But after we no longer experience the world in terms of physical and mental structures, the terms have done much of their deconstructive work. They can be set aside, and if there is a need for them later, we can turn back to them. This process of using a technique and then setting it aside after it has done its job has a long and venerable history in nondual traditions. It is usually called "sublation."

So when we set aside the notion of thoughts, feelings and sensations, we might benefit from a more neutral term that doesn't imply psychological structures lurking in the background. Sometimes I call the comings and goings simply: "arisings."

Arisings are never experienced to occur anywhere other

than in awareness. They never occur outside of awareness for the same reason that in everyday talk, we would say that it's impossible for a thought to appear outside of awareness. Even in everyday talk, it is part of what we mean by "thought" that it is naturally and logically connected to the mind or to a person's local and separate awareness. Thoughts are not separate from awareness even in science fiction movies. This same organic connection goes for *all* objects of awareness (which can also be called "arisings"). In fact, even if we defined a special kind of arising that occurs outside the scope of awareness, a logical impossibility pops up to prove us wrong. Let's say we define a "special arising XYZ that is able to occur outside of awareness." But here comes the impossibility: as soon as that arising comes within the scope of definition, it comes within the scope of awareness. There is no other place for the arising to be. In fact, since awareness is not geographical, the very notion of awareness as a *place* or *locale* dissolves.

When arisings occur, they appear to witnessing awareness in a serial stream. They arise, abide, and subside, one after another. Sometimes there are gaps in between. And through it all, awareness is present. You, as this awareness, are continuous and unbroken even if no arisings are present. The clearest experience of this is deep sleep. No arisings appear during deep sleep, yet it never seems as though you are absent. It never seems as though you stopped existing at the onset of deep sleep, and began existing again upon waking. Rather, it seems in a sweet and subtle way that you are continuous throughout.

Of course your "presence" is not an object. It is not the same kind of presence as an arising has. An arising seems to be able to be present, and then later not be present. But you as awareness aren't present in this way. As awareness, you don't arise, and you can never be absent. You aren't present like a student in roll call. Rather, your nature as awareness is *presence* itself.

Arisings are inert

Besides coming and going, arisings don't actually do anything. They have no causal power. Higher reason has established that arisings aren't physical or mental objects, because physical and mental things themselves are nothing more substantial than arisings in witnessing awareness. As inert comings and goings, arisings are spontaneous and independent of each other. They don't have any power to do anything. Arisings don't enclose or contain each other. They don't cause each other. They don't see each other. They don't refer to each other. They don't touch each other. None of these actions is ever experienced to happen. They are only believed to happen. But beliefs are themselves only thoughts, which are nothing more than arisings. In fact, all of these relationships, such as containing, causing, seeing, referring or touching, are nothing other than arisings themselves. And all of them appear and subside in witnessing awareness.

Sometimes it seems almost irresistible to think of arisings in awareness along the lines of thoughts in the mind. So it can seem as though certain arisings appear all too often, or that they serve as triggers for other ones. But arisings have no power of their own. Power is a kind of concept which is itself another arising in awareness. So arisings have no ability to go offstage and make plans to do things.

They don't hide anywhere and return. When they are not present, there's nowhere else that they are. In terms of arisings, when it seems like some of them trigger other ones to appear, it works more like this:

1. Arising A comes and goes.
2. Arising B comes and goes.
3. Arising C comes and goes.
4. Arising D comes and seems to make a claim: "Arising A was a trigger, because it came up then caused B and C to appear.

But notice that claim in D is itself an arising. And but by the time D appears, A, B, and C are no longer in evidence. There is no present proof that they ever occurred.

Witnessing awareness is not personal

The witnessing awareness that all these arisings appear to is not personal. It is not divided up one per person. It can't be, and there are several ways to see this.

One way is to see that awareness has no physical attributes. It simply cannot be divided into pieces. Awareness is what arisings appear to. As such, it has no form, shape, color, texture or location. So there is no way for there to be more awareness in some places than in others. Awareness has no density, so there can't be more of it inside a person's head than in the middle of the Mojave Desert.

Another way to see that awareness is not personal is to see that there is nothing independently available that can serve as a dividing substance or principle. If we think that awareness is spatially compartmentalized by the bones in a cranium, we have not thoroughly realized that skulls and bones are physical objects that are experienced as thoughts or sensations (arisings) which appear to witnessing awareness.

Sometimes nondual teachings attempt to account for the world of multiplicity by saying that objectless awareness had a desire to experience itself in a new way, and so created the entire phenomenal world of individual perceivers and enjoyers. This can be an effective teaching early on. It can help the student feel a connection between awareness and world of objects so that nothing seems totally disconnected or alienated from awareness.

But later it is less helpful. Notice that this particular creation story gives suspiciously human characteristics to awareness, such as boredom, desire, and production. But our love for awareness has made us want to discover its deeper secrets, and higher reason has allowed us to experience human characteristics as arisings in awareness. As arisings *in* awareness, they simply have no power of their own to serve as individuating principles that *divide* awareness. A drawing of a fissure cannot divide the land.

Higher reason comes to realize that any candidate that seems as though it personalizes awareness is instead already internal to awareness as an arising. Awareness is infinitely more subtle than space, and is whole, unbroken and continuous.

Realizing the witness

You have realized the witness when nothing seems like it is other than awareness. You no longer have that feeling that there is awareness, and also things existing independently of awareness. Even violence, sickness, and biological death don't seem external to awareness. They don't seem like self-constituted, independent things made out of something external to awareness. They don't seem to endanger awareness.

At this point, higher reason has almost finished all the work it can do. The gross world, the subtle world, the body and mind no longer seem as though they exist outside of awareness.[2] Nothing is experienced as a self-sustaining, independent thing, but rather as made of spontaneous arisings in witnessing awareness.

Having realized the witness, you discover that you've always been home. You no longer feel that you were born, or that you will die. If the universe itself perishes, you as awareness are there.

---

2. Together, the gross and subtle worlds, the body and mind are meant to be exhaustive. They are a way to include everything that anyone might think could exist. The gross world would be the world of physical objects, including the cosmological universe, planet earth, rocks, buildings, trees, configurations of the brain and body. The subtle world could be called the world of the subtle energies, auras, entities such as angels, deities and bodhisattvas, heavens and hells, past and future reincarnated lives, dream objects and locations. One could also include abstract things such as logic, mathematics, quantum physics, causality, meaning, language, good, evil, temporality, and all relations. The mind would be all thoughts, feelings, emotions, sensations, memories, values, and states such as swoons, trances, and meditative states such as samadhis, etc. Of course physicists, shamans and accountants would not agree on the composition of these lists. That's OK. The important thing for my purposes is that no candidate for an existent object is in principle omitted. Think of the list in that way!

You don't take any of this personally, because the structures that allowed this are seen never to have existed. You no longer feel lonely, separate or alienated in any way at all. You no longer compare your own spiritual attainments to those of another. You no longer wish to have another's experience, since it no longer seems that experience is in any way personal. Experience has become another term for this same global awareness.

Your experience is utterly sweet and open. The earlier descriptions of awareness as love now fully agree with your direct experience at every moment. It's not that sweetness is experienced as arisings which are pleasant. The sweetness is much deeper than that. It is not an arising object. Rather, sweetness is globally felt as the very source and nature of the arisings. Even arisings that would normally be called "pain" are lovingly held as sweetness by this very same sweetness. Nothing is felt to be an exception to this perfect openness, clarity, love and sweetness. This is radical and revolutionary. And it is your natural state.

The peaceful collapse into pure consciousness

When the witness becomes thoroughly established, it actually begins to evaporate into pure consciousness. Pure consciousness is awareness unconditioned by any witness aspect. It is awareness without the coming and going of arising objects.

One can wait until the dissolution happens. There is no reason to hurry, because there is no suffering, and the witness is sweetness itself. But certain very subtle dualities do remain inherent in the witness. One may wait for their dissolution to happen, or one may feel called by higher reason to investigate the dualities. Either way is fine. If one finds oneself called to investigate, it is a continuation of the sweetness that is already the source of all experience. Any investigation that happens is a further consequence of falling in love with awareness. For one taking this route, the overall question is something like this, "If awareness is nondual like the classic texts and teachers proclaim, then why the appearance of duality?" *Using higher reason, you investigate arisings in the very same way you earlier investigated physical objects, forms, seeing and thoughts.* You scrutinize the seeming duality to see if it is actually warranted by experience.

The duality inherent in the witness may be characterized in several ways:

- It seems as though there is a duality between subject and object. It seems like this duality provides structure to experience. In other words, it seems that there are arisings and witnessing awareness to which they appear. This is felt very sweetly and lightly. It is vastly different from the substantial and heavy dualism that one had felt earlier, when it seemed that minds and bodies were made out of something other than awareness. This duality is very subtle. One knows that arisings can't be anything other than awareness because there is no place else for them to be. This is a bit indirect. It feels this way because the subject/object distinction, which is a very basic duality, has not yet dissolved.

- It seems as though there is a duality between arisings. It seems that arisings come and go. It seems that there are many arisings happening in a serial stream.

Even though one feels confident that they are nothing other than awareness, they still seem to come in a multiplicity. This is a sweet, light and loving situation, but it is not nondual.

Using higher reason, you may investigate in several ways, any one of which can resolve the issue. Basically, the process is the same as you have used all along. You come to find out that it makes no sense whatsoever to consider arisings to be independent. In fact, you come to see that they can't really arise unless they are independent. Since they can't possibly be independent, then it makes no sense to consider that they arise in the first place.

You can investigate the notion of arising itself. How does it seem possible for something to arise inside awareness if it can't possibly ever arise outside of awareness? You may investigate the aspect of time, because it seems that the arisings happen over time. If time isn't something real, then it must itself be an arising. If that is true, then how does that realization affect the structure of the serial stream of arisings?

Or one can examine memory. Memory is a lot less abstract than the nature of an arising or the nature of time! In fact, in *Atma Darshan* Sri Atmananda refers to this approach more than any other to help dissolve the subtle structure of the witness.

Let's try a final experiment with higher reason, using memory as our key ingredient.

Experiment to collapse the witness

Let's take a look at the structure of the witness in the same way we earlier looked at the teacup and at our arm.

Sit comfortably, allowing yourself a deep, slow breath or two. Don't try to think about anything in particular. Don't try to *not* think about anything either. Let arisings come and go. If they repeat, let them repeat. If nothing comes up, that's fine too. Either way; nothing is preferred.

Let the whole stream of arisings continue. Let what comes come. Let what goes go...

At some point, remember a previous arising – perhaps an arising that you would earlier have called a "thought." Try to remember one that was clear and maybe even vivid. Remember it. If you can, hold it there.

Notice that the thought that is being remembered is not actually present. What is present is the memory, which is another thought. The present memory-thought is different from the remembered thought. It is present, and the remembered thought is not present. Try to feel this.

Now try to picture the arising of that previous thought. When it arose, the memory-thought was not present. Try to feel this.

Notice that the two thoughts or arisings are never present at the same time. When the original thought arose, the memory-thought wasn't yet present. And when the memory-thought arises, the remembered thought is no longer present.

The two thoughts or arisings never touch each other. The memory claims to refer to the previous thought, but the previous thought is not present to substantiate the claim. There is actually no proof, no direct experience that the previous thought ever arose. If memory cannot prove the existence of a previous thought, it is not really memory.

Now continue with what seems to be the stream of thoughts. Notice that without memory to make claims about the past, there is never any proof of a thought other than the current thought, right now. Even the supposed multiplicity of thoughts is merely the claim of a single thought, making claims without corroborating proof. There's no proof or direct experience of there being even two thoughts. There can't be two thoughts. Try to feel this.

This leads to something altogether radical. If there can't be two thoughts, it doesn't make sense that there is even *one thought*! The present thought isn't anywhere else when it's not occurring. It doesn't go into hiding in some other location. It can't truly be absent in the usual sense. So then it makes no sense to regard it as present even now. To be able to be either present or absent from awareness, the thought would have to be able to be independent of awareness. But independence is not experienced, and makes no sense. It makes no sense that you are witnessing a thought before you. There is no proof. So it's actually not a thought or arising in the first place. What is going on right now is only awareness. The subject/object structure cannot sustain itself, and collapses peacefully into pure consciousness. Try to feel this...

Witnessing awareness collapses peacefully into pure consciousness when it is realized that the witness is just as dualistic as walking up to the Eiffel Tower and giving it a kick. The witness is much more subtle, but just as dualistic. The witness was a structure consisting of a seer and a multiplicity of things seen. But it was realized that this structure wasn't verified by experience.

Pure awareness or consciousness has no parts, no gaps, no distinctions and no functions. Unlike the witness, it doesn't even have the function of illuminating arising objects. There is no difference between seer and seen, and no arising objects. Your experience as pure consciousness is unbroken in every way. Pure consciousness is full, radiant presence. Pure consciousness shines in its own glory. It is the being of you and the world.

* * *

This is the story of how your love of awareness can enlist the help of higher reason to reveal the secrets of awareness. As Sri Atmananda has said, you have harmoniously blended the head and the heart in peace. You are free, even from the teaching itself. There is great eye-twinkling joy in this!

Dialogues

The Direct Path

Tell me more about the direct path.

This is Sri Atmananda's phrase – "the direct path to Truth."
In it, your nature as nondual awareness is emphasized at the
very start. There is no ignorance to shed, no transformation to undergo, no special emotional experience required
to certify an end state. He opposes it to the "progressive
path," in which you progress gradually towards an intended
final state.

How does one do it?

By being and seeing. Your stand as awareness is a way of
looking at the mind, body, actions and world from the stand-
point of awareness, which is what you already are. This is
the "being" part. You come to see that your every experience
naturally and effortlessly confirms your nature as awareness,
and the stand dissolves. This is the "seeing" part.

Isn't this a bit presumptuous, taking a stand as awareness?

It's not like practicing medicine without a license. You already are awareness. It's a case of standing up for your birthright.

This sounds great; it almost sounds too easy, in fact. How does one actually go about it?

When you do your inquiry and examine objects such as the items in the world, or thoughts, or the self you take yourself to be, have you noticed that you look in different ways? When you see a coffee cup, you are taking a stand as a person. When you see the coffee cup as a visual subtle image, you are taking a stand as a mind to which senses communicate information. This stand is more subtle. It is a step in the right direction. And when you realize how all senses and thoughts require awareness in order that they be seen, how they cannot possibly be seen without awareness, you are taking your stand as this witnessing awareness itself.

This sounds deep. Do I do it all the time, like when I'm driving a car?

It is something you begin to do at the times you normally inquire. You come to see that its effects blossom out to include all of life. It leaves you free for everyday activities.

While driving a car, you don't need to think about any of this – you just drive the car! During your inquiry, take your stand as awareness and see if it is really true that you as a person really drove a car... See what your experience confirms.

OK, then what?

You will see that the person, the car, the driving, were all objects arising in awareness itself. That you are awareness not only while taking your stand but that you are awareness all the time. You will see that you were never anything else; you will see that there is nothing else to be made of. You will stop believing and feeling as though you are something other than awareness. It is this simple.

This really does sound direct.

Yes, awareness is present as your nature from the very beginning. Being it, you see as it.

Your Experience

*W*hat *is your experience like?*

There is no identification of a "your" or "my" in it. I don't see a gap between me and my experience. I don't see myself as "having" experience. Being and experience are inseparable.

No, I mean is it nondual? Is it happy? Is it better than mine?

Many people ask this. They look for a teacher who they feel has more blissful experiences than they do. Then they hang around, trying to get the same for themselves. They interpret experience in a personal way, and they are interested mainly in the emotional or affective component.

Sometimes the teacher encourages this message. But this comes from arrogance and a sense of separation on the teacher's part, from thinking that he or she is different from or better than the student. The age-old message of self-inquiry is not about emotions or feelings or interpersonal comparisons, but about knowing yourself. When one knows one's self as awareness, the basis for interpersonal comparison has evaporated.

Yes, I've heard this…

But if you, seeing yourself as a person, desire more pleasant feelings, there are many ways to proceed. Eat healthy foods, get plenty of sleep and exercise, think good thoughts, and treat people well. These are the things that grandmothers tell their grandkids. It's common sense that still holds true.

Meditation helps as well. Two quick examples. There is an emotional high and an expanded feeling from doing chanting meditation. The feeling is even greater if the chanting is in a tradition where you feel attracted to the symbols and images. Also, there is a heart-opening feeling from the Buddhist *metta* meditation, where you direct the wish for happiness and well-being first to yourself, and then to wider and wider groups of people and beings, including all the sentient beings in all universes everywhere. The benefits from these meditations are tangible and immediate. You always feel better, lighter, more open and more loving afterwards. And the more you do them, the less you do them for your own benefit, and the longer the benefits last.

But what the ancient wisdom teachings talk about is something else.

Yes, but I want my experience to be lastingly blissful and nondual. Like yours and like the satsang teachers I hear, and Ramana's and Nisargadatta's experience.

Part of the reason you have this requirement is that you imagine others being separate but in this same state. But this isn't what they say about themselves. It isn't even what they're talking about. Ramana and Nisargadatta – not only are they not talking about emotional, phenomenal feeling states, but they are also not personalizing experience. The pointer given by all these teachings is not personal. The pointer directs you to see through the presumption of the separate person. The person cannot withstand inquiry. So it is not the person's experience they are talking about.

Then what are they talking about? I thought Ramana and Nisargadatta were talking about themselves.

Nisargadatta did speak later in his life of the pain. This is a clue that he wasn't speaking about blissful feeling states...

Yeah, what about an experience of pain? Isn't that a case of suffering in experience?

Experience is the vast, edgeless clarity in which things seem to arise. It possesses no point of view or stake in things. Maybe it seems like experience is "yours" – but actually everything you can point to that feels like "you" is an arising in experience.

What do you mean?

Look at your hand... Now close your eyes and allow your hand to rest on your knee... It probably seems like it's your hand. But everything you can say about it is based on a thought, or image, a kinesthetic feeling, or a belief. These thoughts and feelings aren't tied down to an owner. They are not located or centered, but float free in awareness. There is nothing about these feelings, and nothing in awareness, that makes any of it "yours." There is no tie to a person. The person is not the experiencer; the person is experienced.

How can I know that? It seems like I have a definite stake in things. Because I want, what did you say? – the "edge…"

Edgeless clarity?

Yes! Once I hear something like this, it feels natural to want it for myself.

Yes it does. This is natural as long as you take yourself to be a container of experience. It seems to you that experience is something that happens inside you, and that other people have their own experiences inside them. But it is the other way around. Your body, your mind, and everything identifiable about you are experienc-ed, witness-ed. Body, mind, thoughts, values and memories are all objects. The clarity is the light within which they arise.

Wow! It's like backwards. But is this something I can see?

You're seeing it now! Actually, all seeing is it. You can't possess it, because it is the space within which you appear. It's like the airline passenger wanting to hold up the plane, when the plane is holding up the passenger.

Ah, I felt a shift there… But a moment later, when I think about it a little, it doesn't seem like that to me.

Don't try to reason it out. Stand farther back for a moment

and be open... The person is something you seem to observe as if from a small distance. You aren't actually the skull, mind, body or memories of the person – those are objects that are observed. You are what they appear to – that global experience, that openness, within which things seem to arise. The body, the mind, even the entire person seems to arise within this openness. The openness is you, which is why it seems that "you" notice things arising.

But why aren't all my experiences like these close, direct ones you mention?

These seemingly close, direct experiences are teaching pointers for what is now and always the case. All experience is always direct – there is no partition or mediation, no veil, and no subject/object split.

OK, but can you explain how that is "always" the case?

There is never any subject/object split in the first place. The "split" is part of a story that has become a habit. The notion of the split and the feeling of being at a distance from objects can actually fall away, and experience recaptures its original, global and unbroken beauty.

How can I make it fall away for me?

Have you ever had an experience such as totally getting caught up by a sunset or movie? Where there's no sense of self or other, not even a sense of what is going on at the moment? It seems quite nondual. Sometimes it's called "being in the zone."

Sure.

Look deeply into this sunset experience, and see how all your experience is like this. Even the experiences where you seem to be separate are just like this. Every moment is like this. Even thinking that it is *not* like this, is just like the sunset experience. You are always at one with yourself as awareness right there. Only later does it seem like there was something in particular that you were doing. But even *then*, in the midst of this later "seeming," you are totally there as well.

Ah yes! I can tell you that right now, this *moment sure seems whole and unbroken.*

Yes, it is all like this...

Thank you!

Visit From a Chemist

My friend told me about your conversation last week. But I'd like to know what your experience is like.

Yes, I was telling him that experience isn't "mine." It carries no logo or branding. If you add up all the experiences that seem like they are yours, and set them aside – what is there of you left over to *have* experience? Such a place can't be found. Yet experience is a presence, a global sweetness, unshakable and unbroken.

Yes, I've heard you say this. I've heard others say this kind of thing too. But I just don't get it. With all the talk about awareness and consciousness, it smacks of idealism to me. I'm more a physicalist. Can you explain this in physical terms?

Sure. We can use physical terms. That doesn't mean it's a physical thing. It's not a mental thing either. Experience has no geographical center or preferred substance. Let's say you experience a pain in your leg. It seems to immediately suggest the leg itself. You could say that the leg has a geographical location. But the *experience* of the pain has no location.

I feel that my experience is here.

Right about where you feel your leg to be?

Yes, right here.

OK, let's try this. You are sitting at the table. Shut your eyes and reach your hand out to touch the tabletop.

OK...

Now, the touching itself, the experience itself. Is it behind something? Is it in front of something? Is it to the left or right of something?

Well, the table is right here in front of me. My hand tells me so.

For the moment, I'm not talking about the table or the hand. Your question was about experience – so try to isolate the experience itself. See what's true of it. Is the *experience* in front of you?

(Eyes still closed) *Now I think I understand what you mean. The experience itself isn't in front or in back of anything. It's just kind of there...*

Yes. Does it seem to be inside your body?

No. My body is not really included in the experience. It seems to be just present, just there.

From the vantage point of inside this touching-the-table experience, does it seem like it belongs to *you*?

Again, no. From inside the experience, I have no impression of me.

OK, you can open your eyes. This is what I meant by no "your" or "my" to experience. It is presence, neither personal nor impersonal. You asked how my experience is. Like this. And it is the same for you. It is experience itself.

But when I think about it, lots of stuff comes back, like my body, and the idea that experience is nothing but brain function. You know that I'm a chemistry major!

Yes, but the brain and chemistry, and your web of beliefs are no different. They are just like the table. They are non-located experience. There are just presence – the same way you saw right here.

Yes, I did get a glimpse right there. It certainly doesn't seem like that all the time. Right now, it seems like the brain made me have that experience, and is making me have this one. How can I get that same nonlocated experience all the time like you do?

Do you visually observe the brain creating experience in a particular place? Or is that a story? Your experience, even in the midst of that story, is nonlocated. There is no true location. There is no true entity to occupy any location or to serve as a personal pivot-point for experience.

But how can I really be sure of that?

At some quiet point in the day, take a look at what seem to be your experiences. See if you can find any inherent difference between the experiences that seem located, and the glimpse of nonlocated presence you had. Experience will prove it: everything is like that tabletop moment. Seeing this very clearly will make you more and more unable to take the brain-function story as absolute truth. This in turn will allow you to open into experience itself. It will become your living reality. This is the sweetness I mentioned earlier.

That would be great! But what would it do to my science studies? If science isn't absolutely true, then what should I do? Change my major?

There's no need to change your major! No story is absolutely true – that is, no story is a more realistic image of a storyfree reality. Science, law, folklore, medicine, religion – none of it. Even our conversation here. Instead of regarding these concepts as accurate or inaccurate representations of a reality outside of concepts, allow the assumed border between inside and outside to melt away. All of these fields of study are stories or songs, interwoven webs that arise within the globality of experience itself. Chemistry is just like this – it's a very helpful story. It relates to other stories, such as creating new medicines and computer chips. If you don't change your major, maybe you will create a new medicine. That would be a nice story! None of this requires you to believe chemistry to be a representational truth. That belief is misleading, unnecessary, and leads to feelings of separation.

(A few seconds later) *Wow! I got a jolt right there, like a flash of insight. But now it's gone. Let me think about this for a while…*

So Now – How Should I Talk?

Yesterday I had a deep experience that everything is borderless space. I just knew it. And then of course I came back to my normal kind of experience. But now I don't think that anything I see or hear is the truth anymore. I feel that I am not being true to my realization by the kind of talk that goes on day to day.

Sometimes it's confusing to encounter nondual teachings. Many varieties of nondual teachings seem to imply that there is simply no free will, no mind, no people and no objects. So we wonder how to talk without "backsliding." If the teachings are then taken at face value, what about those mundane things like paying taxes, raising children, eating dinner and getting a haircut? Do we somehow stop doing these things now that we've ingested a teaching that says they aren't what they seem, that they don't truly exist?

So, is there a way I should talk now?

No. Any cosmically grounded "shoulds" have vanished. Talk as you please. There's no need for a "nondually correct" way to speak. There's no fixed, objective world out there to become indignant if you describe it in the "wrong" terms! There *are* no wrong terms! In speaking, you are free from the limitation of "getting the world right." Follow your heart. Sometimes people begin their relationship to teachings by adopting a new vocabulary, trying it on for size. You might find a delight in the words, or a resonance with a beloved teacher speaking those words. The teachings might then grow to become clearer through inference or demonstration, or even a spontaneous, noninferential experience. And then at some point it is unshakably realized that experience was never truly characterized by duality or separation in the first place.

At this point, what had been felt as a difference between "appearance" and "reality" collapses. It no longer seems like there is an "accurate" or "inaccurate" way to "represent" things. Speech is no longer seen as a mirror of reality, but becomes free and unveiled.

But Ramana and Nisargadatta and Buddha never spoke about paying taxes or getting a haircut...

This is because virtually every word you have ingested from these teachers was recorded and extracted from teaching contexts. It's not so common to chatter about one's hygiene or personal finances while surrounded by people and conversing about nonduality... It becomes a matter of language and context. Multilingual people don't speak the same language or dialect all the time in every situation. A physicist might devote his life to scientific research, but you can be sure he doesn't tell the traffic cop, "I didn't run a red light, because subatomic particles are all there is."

But I feel that I'm falling back into duality by speaking normally.

You can't slip into duality, which is the false claim that the world is made of many separate things truly separate from you. You can't create duality by speaking. There is freedom in this. Once you know the truth of yourself, you will feel this freedom from falling.

Imagine you are telling a friend about your vacation. You want to say how you went to Paris and saw the Eiffel Tower. But then you know that there are truly no external, separate objects to see, and no individual, located point of view where seeing comes from. There is truly no separate seer. And you know that in nondual circles people often speak in a way that doesn't assume the reality of these things. And you've read how Ramana and Papaji and other famous teachers have encouraged seekers to ask, *"Who* did this, *who* said this?"* So you are tempted to say something like, *"This form appeared to travel and was merged into the Paris form. In the illusory passage of time, the Eiffel Tower form appeared. There was the illusion of excitement in this form."* But there's no need to speak like this all the time, especially once you have inquired and discovered the truth. You know the inseparability of you as awareness from all that arises within it, including cities and structures, you will not feel as though one way of speaking is more nondually correct than other ways of speaking.

Words may even come to you more lightly and fluidly than before. Actions as well. There's no conflict, no back-sliding, no falling into anything by using everyday language instead of talk of appearance, form and borderless space.

So it's OK to speak in terms of "things"...

Sure, we're doing it now! In the Jewish, Advaitin, and Buddhist teachings, there is a profound insight: Not believing in things, yet speaking the language of things.

"Thing-talk" is a kind of conceptual and social shorthand that makes life smoother. Refusing to use thing-talk leads to foolishness. And not crazy-wisdom, sagelike foolishness, but Beavis 'n' Butthead slacker-foolishness: "Pay my restaurant check? No way – that would require separation, and there isn't any separation."

This almost sounds as if you're trying to impress upon others that you have a deep realization. There's a name for that kind of talk – Lucknow Disease.[3]

So there's no conflict, nothing gets created in this way...

That's right. And you don't fall back. Insights don't reverse themselves just because you use everyday speech. You won't lose points. No one is keeping score. Contexts have different vocabularies. In chemistry lab, you might use the "everything-is-particles" vocabulary. In court testifying as a witness you might use everyday observational terms. While discussing meditation and relaxing into space, you'll

---

3. Lucknow Disease is a linguistic malady first observed in Lucknow, India in the early 1990s. It is characterized by avoidance of the "I-word" – presumably to demonstrate to one's self and others that there is no longer any ego or sense of self here. Instead of using the word "I" in sentences, Lucknow Disease sufferers say things like "This form is going to the bathroom." The irony of Lucknow Disease is that it strikes only when the person's sense of self is present and poorly integrated. It has never been observed in those whose sense of self is well-integrated – or absent.

perhaps use some yogic, advaitic, spiritual and geometric terms. In psychology class you might use the language that allows for choice, cognition and willed action.

In a Philosophy 101 class, you argue about the existence of choice, but in an Ethics 101 class, or ordering food at a diner(!), choice is most often assumed, so the talk is a bit different.

All of these different language-groupings have their ways, their consistency and coherence. Only if you expect one vocabulary to truly represent all situations are you faced with the sense of fundamental incompatibilities or the need to reconcile different situations under a common neutral description. Without this expectation, language and thought are free.

Is Consciousness Nondual?

*M*any *teachers say that consciousness is nondual. Isn't this conclusion just conceptual? It seems like each one of us has a separate consciousness.*

Yes, it is conceptual. Any statement is conceptual. "Dual." "Nondual." These kinds of statements depend on concepts of consciousness, nonduality, duality, "is-ness," and so forth. You say "just" conceptual. As opposed to what? Conceptual as opposed to actually *true*?

Yes, I want to know what consciousness actually is, *like what's really true about it. Some teachers say that nondual consciousness is objectless. Others say that it is knowledge knowing itself. But that seems like a subject/object kind of thing, not very nondual! So, bottom line: nondual consciousness – which is it, objectless or self-knowing?*

"Objectless." "Self-knowing." Both are metaphors of slightly different flavors. They aren't meant to be taken literally. These metaphors take advantage of the fact that most people feel that experience is divided. The metaphors are meant to indicate a way of experience that isn't divided. Once that "happens," that is, once experience no longer seems divided, then you won't distinguish between "consciousness" and "other than consciousness." The very notion of consciousness will gently and peacefully dissolve. And yet you may find yourself using the "consciousness" word, but again, lightly, with no metaphysical baggage attached.

But I've heard of direct, nondual, experiential knowing. I'd like to know nondual consciousness in this way.

Yes, this is exactly what I just described. You are looking to behold it directly, correct? In such a way that it embraces you and you embrace it, and there is nothing left out, correct?

That's right!

It's already happening! You inescapably know this consciousness in a nondual way by being it. It's not the way the mind knows "2+2=4" or "Sacramento is the capital of California." It's not an objective knowing, because there are no objects in it. It's not the kind of thing you can stand away from and look at from the side. Knowing consciousness is not like looking at the headlights of a car.

Well, why do some teachers speak of "knowing it"? It sounds like some people know it and others don't.

And you'd like to be one of the knowers, correct? (*smiles*)

Yes. There must be something to that. You've gotta admit, lots of writings mention this. What are they talking about?

"Knowing it" means losing the confusion that you might actually be something else. It means to no longer take yourself as a person, as an object. In the West it's called gnosis. In the East it's said that you know it by being it. In both cases, it's a discovery made by the mind about something that was always the case – that you are awareness itself. You are not a separate object, absolutely cut off from the world. The ironic thing is this – as soon as you "know" it, you see that "knowing" was impossible. The kind of thing to which people attribute "knowing" is a mind, a brain, or a person. But you have realized that these are only objects. Objects can't "know" anything. A "mind" can't know anything for the same reason that a "teacup" can't know anything – it is an object. In fact, knowingness itself is an object. You also have seen that there are truly no separate objects at all, so there can be no separate "knowers."

Oh, I see what you mean about knowing. It doesn't make sense to require myself to "know" something like this. But I would still like to not take myself as a person.

You would like to lose the belief, the feeling, that you are a person?

That's right! I will feel less anguish then. Many teachers say that suffering comes from this belief.

OK, but notice that you are asking as a person. Having beliefs and losing beliefs is the kind of thing that persons do. Nondual awareness doesn't "do" anything.

OK, so what's wrong with that?

Nothing! In fact it's normal to see this in a personal way. Until you don't...

OK, later maybe I'll understand it. But right now I must admit there's the feeling of wanting to lose this belief, no matter what it is properly called.

To lose this belief, become curious about what you are really made of. Be true to your own experience and find out whether you actually *are* a person.

Find out – how?

Look very deeply. Investigate the claim that you are a person by investigating the consequences of this claim. If the consequences do not bear up to your direct experience, then neither does the claim itself. For example, if you really are a person, then wherever you are, the person will be too. Is this true? Are you ever there when the person is not? Is the person ever there when the seer of the person is not? Look for the usual parts that make up the person. The body, the mind, values, emotions, memories and anything else included in the person. If you are there when these things are not present, then they can't be the sum and substance of what you are.

Can you give me an example of how I go about it?

Deep sleep is the best example. During deep sleep, according to your experience, is your body present in experience during deep sleep?

It must be there.

But is it experienced? In deep sleep, do you see it, feel it, hear it or sense it?

No...

So in that moment, according to your experience, can it be said to be present?

No.

Are YOU there? Do you sense that you were absent? Look back on the experience of deep sleep. Does it now seem like you had gone out of existence? Or does it seem like you were present the whole time?

It seems that I am like the body... I didn't see the body in deep sleep. And I didn't see or hear myself either.

Good observation! But the YOU that I am asking about is the witnessing awareness. This is the nondual consciousness you asked about earlier. Did this witnessing awareness stop existing during deep sleep, and then begin existing again when you woke up? Or do you sense continuity in it?

Now that you say it like that, I do sense continuity. Like I am not interrupted even through sleep.

So your presence is not interrupted, but the experience of the body as an object *is* interrupted?

Right, because the body is not experienced at that time…

So the body cannot define what you are. Because you are present when the body is not.

I see. I never thought about it that way, but it's true!

This is an example of how you come to realize that you aren't a person. You come to see that you aren't defined by the components of the person. You see how they are intermittent appearances, while you are never absent. Deeply seeing this will shed the notion that you are the person. That notion will make as much sense as believing that you are a pair of jeans.

Ah, yes! Where can I go from here?

Look for the mind as well. Other than a succession of thoughts, can you find the mind at all? Test the findings against your experience, not against a theory about what ought to be the case. Do you really experience the presence of the mind? If you can't find the mind, then how can the mind be what you are? This investigation can be carried out with every candidate, every component that you think *might* be you. See what happens. This is self-inquiry – finding out who you truly are.

How Are Objects a Block?

You've written that the notion that physical objects are external is a block to nondual inquiry. Can you say more about that?

Using objects in everyday activities does not block your inquiry. You can actually put on your clothes in the morning or drink a cup of coffee and do inquiry at the same time. But it is a block to take objects literally as external, independent, solid chunks of reality separated from yourself. If you regard objects as separate, then you regard yourself as separate. This sense of separation is based on these unwarranted object-beliefs, and gains a false conviction from kinesthetic experiences and the feelings of bodily muscular contractions. In truth, however, the body is not separate. It is unlimited and infinitely light, as awareness. The body is not in space, it is infinitely more subtle than space. It is awareness itself.

But we tend to think in spatial, physicalist terms, and use these terms widely. The spatial concept of physical separation tends to serve as the paradigm for *all* our notions of difference. We tend to experience "difference" as spatial. This makes us think of two aspects existing on opposite sides of unbridgeable spatial gaps. Examples include feeling cut off from reality (as in "it's out there, we're in here"), feeling cut off from other people, feeling separated from our goals and the objects of our desires, and feeling ourselves to be divided in various ways: heart from mind, mind from body, conscious from subconscious, worldly from spiritual, etc. We almost feel as though these things occupy different places. And all of these feelings make us experience ourselves as all alone, vulnerable, and perishable.

But isn't this the way things really are?

No. You never experience spatial externality or independence. Instead, you merely accept a story about it. This can be demonstrated. Try this: Shut your eyes. Now try to just listen... air-conditioning sounds... hushed conversational sounds... clinking silverware and coffee cup sounds... diner sounds. But there's no evidence of an external air conditioner or cup appearing as such. In fact, the sound is the only appearance. In this moment, outside the sound, you don't have evidence of a true external air-conditioner or cup.

But where is the sound itself located? The sound is not on the outside or inside. It's not on the left, right, north or south. There is no dividing line between the sound and you. Of course there might be a story line that makes an existential claim about the sound. This story line might say that the cup is physically located "outside." But notice that this "outside" is not evident in the sound itself.

This is the same for all the senses. Try this with vision. Place two similar coffee cups in front of you. Now, attend to the visual evidence alone. Two cylindrical patches of white, with Formica-beige between them... No line between the colors and you... No evidence in the colors of being "out there" ... There is no evidence of yourself being an observer "in here." Nevertheless, based on these colors and their change over time, we conclude that there are objects external to us. We accept a story that these objects are separated from us. But there's no support for this story in the visual evidence itself.

OK, so are you saying there are no cups or people?

Not independent from experience. Not as separate from you. It is not your experience that things exist in and of themselves, apart from experience. Think about the way you experience a cup. It is not apart from seeing or touching or thinking. Seeing, hearing, touching and thinking are never present without awareness within which they arise. It's all awareness all the time. And awareness is the very nature of you.

You never experience an unexperienced cup. You might think you do experience a cup that is in itself an unexperienced object. This is what classical Western science has taught. Heisenberg began to show how experience itself conditions the supposed object of experience. Experience is always in the makeup of anything experienced. There's never experience of something existing apart from experience. So this whole notion of independent existence can be dropped as incoherent and productive of feelings of separation.

So, what's left?

Experience, which is always whole and non-separate. And when it doesn't seem like there's anything other than experience, then it won't seem like there's a real thing called experience either. Existence/nonexistence, being and non-being will stop making sense and will drop away, no longer serving as partitions. You'll never feel cut off from the world again.

Well, I sure seem to experience this chair, this pencil, this cup of coffee. What is it like not to have any experience of these things?

Free, light, weightless, uncrowded, unburdened, sweet and peacefully present.

Like really connected...

Ah! No, I don't mean like Dustin Hoffman tried to illustrate with his white towel in *I Heart Huckabees* – "Everything's connected!" It's closer than that, much closer. There's neither a feeling of connection or disconnection with the chair and pencil. It's all present, here, now. There's not an impression of the pencil as something on the other side of some spatial relation.

No spatial relations. How is that possible in the physical world? I hear you ride a bike. How do you explain that?

In fact, I ride a bike with no gears and no brakes. It's called a track bike. The lightness I'm speaking of actually makes the track bike easier to ride than it would have been, even on city streets. By the way, there are many others who ride the same kind of brakeless bikes. I've spoken with many of them over the years. Even though they have no interest in these spiritual kinds of inquiries, they often report the same lightness, the sense that everything is hooked in together with you the rider. Everything moves and flows together in a way that is light and free and connected.

This just doesn't make sense to me. How light is it if you get hit by a bus!?

The same! I've had accidents, I've been hit by cars, other cyclists and skaters. I've crashed and had bleeding injuries. I've had sprains, damage to the ligaments, and was once not able to ride for 6 months. This is all lightness itself, having zero weight and zero external existence, just like ideas. Injury, damage to the body, pain – they're all lightness.

So it's all in the mind then?

No, because without an outside, how can there be an inside? It's more that there's no border.

How can someone come to experience this?

By coming to see that all experience is whole as it is, and not disconnected from you. Experience doesn't indicate objects outside of experience, so there's no gap. One key to this is not to associate unpleasantness or pain with disconnection. Allow these to be as they are without making symbols or metaphors out of them.

Personal Identity

How does all this talk about physical objects relate to self-inquiry? After all, I don't think I am a physical object. I also know I am not this coffee cup in front of me. But you've spoken of not seeing objects, and I want to experience what you experience.

I experience no edges or borders or limits. I cannot experience a difference between "me" and "you." Your inquiry will confirm this as "your" experience as well. It is not personal, but global, unlimited. It is already that. That is, inquiry will reveal the lack of difference between a "you" and an "other." Ironically, the desire to attain this as a personal experience is as close to separation as you'll ever get – and even then it is not truly separate. The desire to experience what another experiences is based on unsubstantiated beliefs, all of which lead to suffering. Wanting to experience what we project "an enlightened person" experiences is the very feeling of suffering; it's not the path to the ending of suffering.

How so?

When this desire arises, do you feel more together, or more separate?

Definitely more separate, but wanting to be together.

OK, let's look into it. You say you don't think you are a physical object. Yet you'd like to experience what I experience. This is because you haven't fully let go of the idea that you are a physical object. You see us as two separate places where experience happens. But if there are no physical objects, then how can there be separate experiencers? You see, there's no way to make this distinction between experiencers without distinguishing them by physical characteristics.

This distinction between experiencers depends on a sense that experiencing is rooted, centered and located. And how can you localize something without treating it as a physical object? Other than the concepts of shape, boundary, extension, left/right, here/there, how can one center be marked off from another? You might not have the explicit belief that you are a physical object like a body, but in a subtle way you are still granting independent existence to physical objects.

I'm not aware of treating experiencers as physical objects. Can you explain a bit more?

You say that you would like to experience what I experience, correct?

Yes...

But you see, any characteristic you come up with that seems to distinguish one "center of experience" from another will be a physical characteristic. Here/there, right/left, this side of the room/that side of the room. Any dividing line is based on physical properties such as line, extension, shape, contiguity to other shapes.

Yet any shape or line is merely the interface between two colors, which are nothing more than ideas. This is the same for any characteristic. Shapes are nothing other than ideas. Not just visually but even felt shapes like the shape of an arm or coffee cup are ideas. The shape is not apart from the feeling of the shape, and the feeling is not apart from awareness of the feeling. It's all awareness, all the time. This is how there are no separate physical objects. So how can there be separate experiencers?

So I can't be in your shoes, right?

You aren't in any shoes, even now. The shoes are in you, which is awareness.

The desire to have the same thing someone else seems to have makes people think they're missing something. They'd like to have the same kinds of experiences that they believe an "enlightened one" has. And yet enlightenment is the very lack of separateness in the first place. It's across the board. As they would say in Zen, it's just as much in the North as it is in the South. So it cannot be bottled up in one person, leaving the other person without. It can't be owned.

This is wonderfully inspiring! At first it makes me feel peaceful, as though nothing truly is lacking. But then I think, how can I better understand this? I don't really want to think of you and me as really persons, but I still don't think I have the same experiences you do.

Is it like you are thinking of us in a kind of abstract way as different centers of experience, but not really located anywhere?

Yes, that's it!

And in some way, you are there and I am here?

Yeah, something like that...

You asked how to understand this. It's not a matter of taking up a new theory, but seeing your present theory as a story taken literally, taken to the bank. Being invested in that story makes you think you are separate and walled off. Without this structure in the mix, there would be no presumption or experience of separation.

What is that structure you're talking about?

It's the structure underlying the notion of separate centers of experience. We can dismantle the structure by looking at the very notion of "center."

I never thought of that. How would you do it?

OK, let's look into just what you think this center is.

OK...

How are you thinking of a center? What divides one from another? Does it seem like there's a "here" and a "there"?

In a kind of soft way, yes. Like your center is over there, mine is closer to here.

But if there is no body, how are you finding the "here"?

What do you mean?

Can something be to the left of an idea? In front of an idea?

Aaah, no!

So if you have deconstructed your body in that you see it as nothing other than ideas, then how can ideas be close to other ideas or far from them? How can there be ideas over here or over there? How can ideas surround a center? Can you make any sense of that?

Not when you put it in those terms...

Can you put it another way? Can you give sense to the idea of a center without treating it like something related to a physical object?

No, not right now...

So can you see that apart from taking these physicalistic words literally, there is simply no way to conceive of separate centers of experience? Hence the supposed difference between "you" and "me" dissolves.

This is why it is so important to deconstruct the experience of physical objects as objective things, independent of awareness. Our notions of differentiation tend to be based on physical characteristics, such as position or location. Let me ask – to you right now, what is the difference between you and me?

You're sitting over there, and I'm right here.

And this couldn't make any sense unless you thought of yourself, as well as me, as bodies with awareness inside them. The great Advaitin Krishna Menon said that "what we take ourselves to be is what we seem to see." If you take yourself to be a body, then the world seems to be made up of physical objects. If you take yourself to be a mind, then the world seems to be made of subtle essences including minds. And if you take yourself to be awareness, then the world is experienced as nothing but awareness.

But I know I'm not the body – the body changes over time, and I know that I am what watches it, and that I have remained unchanged.

Yet you feel like you are "inside" the body?

Yes – I can see things only from this angle. If I were not inside this body, I would be able to travel anywhere, and see anything from any angle.

Do you feel like you are in any specific location inside the body?

Hmm, let me see...

Do you feel that you are above the waist or below the waist?

Above, definitely.

OK, do you feel you are above the neck or below the neck?

Above the neck.

OK, above the nose or below?

Above.

Can you narrow it down any more?

I feel like I am behind the eyes.

How big are you? What shape?

Oh, about an inch wide, maybe round.

Behind the forehead? On the left, right, or in the center?

I feel like I'm in the center behind the eyes.

How far back from the eyes?

Oh, about an inch.

OK, we've found you!! A marble-sized ball about an inch behind the center of the forehead!

I guess so (smiling)...

Now – what is it that this marble appears to?

What?

Well, as we talk about this, does the little marble seem to appear as an image?

Yes it does!

So if this image is appearing, what is it appearing to? That is, it doesn't seem like the marble is doing the seeing – it seems like the marble is being seen.

Yeah, I understand. The little marble isn't the seer – it is being seen. I guess it's just an idea I have of myself.

Yes, based on a few habitual things, such as the prominence of the visual sense over hearing, taste and smell. Also based on the association that arises over time between thinking of one's self and the subtle muscular contractions in the forehead region. It makes us think that this is where we are.

But now, think of the marble image, and that which is aware of the marble image. If you had to place your true self on one side or the other, would you be on the side that is seeing? Or the side that is being seen?

The seeing side, definitely. I feel that I'm looking at this marble. So how can I be over there inside the marble?

OK, the seeing of the marble – think about this seeing. As the seeing arises, does the seeing have a location?

No, it isn't experienced as being in a location. I can say it must be in the brain, but that's just an idea. The experience itself doesn't have any location at all. Aha!

That's it! Nothing else has a location either. And that awareness in which these arise is your Self. It is the non-separate Self of all.

And in the midst of this realization, there's no desire to experience anything else. It doesn't make sense that experience is anyplace or happening inside anyone.

Wanting an Enlightenment Experience

I read about the life-changing enlightenment events that people write about – and I haven't had one. Does this mean I'm not "done" yet?

What is it that you'd like to be "done" with? Do you want what you're calling an enlightenment event because it might feel good, or to confirm something?

Suffering. I don't want to suffer any more.

How do you visualize this non-suffering?

Like not having any problems anymore.

Life without death? Health without disease? They contain each other. You can't hold a one-ended stick. The famous stories we read are not about life without birth, illness, death, or unpleasantness. How can there be life without its ups and downs? Ramana Maharshi, Nisargadatta Maharaj, Rama-krishna, Suzuki Roshi were all struck with cancer. Many teachers and expositors of profound nondual teachings have had family problems, financial problems, health problems, emotional problems.

OK, then what are they talking about? Nisargadatta had cancer, but he's also famous for saying, "In my world, nothing goes wrong." It makes me want the same thing.

Good point! Depends upon where you, the interpreter, place the "I." If you place the "I" at Nisargadatta, then there was a body, with cancer and pain. If Nisargadatta (or any person) is the center of that world, then there is a lot wrong in it. But if you place the "I" at That which witnesses what occurs, then there is nothing wrong. Nothing happening at all. And nothing missing. It isn't personal. This "I" is the being of Nisargadatta, you, me, all else. This is where the "I" has always been. It is pure and untouched, and always available.

Is there any way I can really see or know this "I"?

You can't see it – it sees you. Awareness sees you. It is happening now, and has always been the case. Just like you see your arm, Awareness sees the body/mind you take as yourself. Just like your own seeming passage from waking to deep sleep and back to waking. In deep sleep, there is no evidence that the world or the body is present. That is, the body can't be said to be there. Yet there's no sense that "you" are ever missing. Your true "I" does not depend on phenomenal activity to be present. Actually, your true I is not really "present" as in the opposite of "absent." Rather, it is Presence itself.

But some people seem to know this, and others don't.

There's no need for this to be known by a person. There is actually no possibility that this can be comprehended or held by a person. Personal grokking is just another coming-and-going experience, like a mood or a runny nose.

I think I understand that, but it doesn't make the desire to know go away...

Yes, this inquiry is about knowing. It's not about feeling or possessing. It's not about having only certain feelings or desires and not others. If you seek this intimate knowledge, then do what so many others have done – inquire deeply into the supposed makeup of a person. Inquire into the makeup of life, death, into that which you consider to be yourself. Inquire into that which would supposedly benefit by "knowing." Be as intensely motivated to look into these matters as you would be to gasp for air after being held under water. Look everywhere. Don't stop if it gets rough. The search is sweet, but it is not always comfortable or reas-suring to the assembly labeled as the person. Be unafraid of what might come up.

And then what?

If this is truly what you want, then you will find it. Two iro-nies. One, when it "happens," you'll see that it really didn't happen. Two, during this inquiry, you weren't looking for "enlightenment"!

I hear what you are saying, but I must admit, I really do feel like I would like to have the same kind of experience I read about others having.

I understand this. Many people feel this way – even those who have been asked to teach by their teachers. One teacher asked my advice on this. He really wanted to have this kind of transcendent mountaintop experience, but he never did. The best he was able to come up with was this – he looked at the history of his seeking. He counted up the peak experiences he had, and they came to about 12 or 13. He wondered, if he added those together, could they equal one large experience? He had internalized a notion that to be a well-known teacher you had to have a dramatic enlightenment story in your toolbox.

Funny, he wasn't interested at all in Buddhism. If he had been, he would have felt better to hear about Shunryu Suzuki, one of the most famous Zen teachers in the English-speaking world. Huston Smith, the famous religious studies scholar, once asked Shunryu Suzuki why satori (i.e., enlightenment experience) didn't figure in Suzuki's famous book *Zen Mind, Beginner's Mind*. Suzuki's wife replied with a smile, "It's because he hasn't had it."

These experiences sometimes called "enlightenment events" are ironic. They never come when you look for them. If they do come, they come while you are looking in another direction entirely. They usually disappear before you get the chance to talk about them! They never last. And nothing is made true or authentic by these experiences. And looking for these experiences actually serves to push them away.

Looking for enlightenment itself is like looking for the golden egg. Instead, look for the goose.

In this case, what is the goose?

The truth of yourself. Once you find it, you won't think of enlightenment in the same way. It won't seem like a special power, a state of being, or a set of qualities.

Seeking special effects will inevitably sidetrack you. The various nondual teachings all agree that these experiences are beside the point. You can have blisses and buzzes without understanding, and vice versa.

Identifying "enlightenment" with a feeling or experience coopts the notion into serving a personal agenda. The same for "being done." But in any of the great descriptions of enlightenment, your freedom is never a personal or political freedom. It's not about being a person free of needs. A person needs air and nutrition and love.

You can see these things poetically, metaphorically. You can see these everyday needs as clues to your nature, as met by your nature as awareness. You are not a person, but the awareness in which the person arises. Awareness doesn't feel these needs because it is not a person. An organism has a need for air, but awareness doesn't have this need – you as awareness are like air itself, totally clear and uninterrupted, without borders. An organism has a need for nutrition, but awareness doesn't have this need – you as awareness are the sustenance of all that appears. A person has the need for love, but awareness doesn't have this need – you as awareness are like love itself, totally open and generous, never saying "no" to anything that arises. There is no requirement to "possess" this in any way. The person is actually "possessed" by this openness, this sustenance and this generosity. No experience proves or establishes this. No experience can overturn it.

Why Wasn't I Enlightened at Satsang?

I have been attending satsangs for years. I've gotten very close to enlightenment. In fact a few times the teacher told me I was actually There. But then it seemed to go away. This has happened to lots of others too. Why?

Many satsang attendees report this. It seems like this experience came, then went, correct?

Yes!

This coming and going is called the "flip-flop." It's one of the main dynamics at most satsangs, as well as their main problem. It is the onset of a very transcendent experience, followed by its departure.

Yes, that's right.

Now at satsang, didn't the teacher tell you that it is not about having an experience?

Yes. They all say that.

And yet you are wondering about the onset and disappearance of an experience.

Uh, I guess so. (smiling sheepishly) *I think it is because at those times, I am in contact with my true nature.*

And at other times, you are not, correct?

Yes, that's right. It is blocked.

This is due to some of the satsang teachings themselves. One well-known teaching is that at some moments there is a direct, experiential, knowing contact with your nature, while at most other times this knowledge is veiled or confused by story, belief, doubt, fear, anger or scattered-mindedness. According to the "veil" teaching, there are certain moments at satsang where the student has heart-opening, oceanic, loving, emotionally blissful experiences. It is taught that during these moments, the normally occluding veils have dropped away, giving the student a direct experience of their true nature. Sometimes it's called a "free sample."

Not all satsangs teach this. It's less common than it used to be, as some of the teachers seem to have recognized problems with it. But the veil teaching sounds familiar, doesn't it?

Yes, this sounds pretty familiar. And I must say, it sounds pretty good, too. Are you saying that something is wrong with it?

It tends to identify the timeless truth of your nature with a coming-and-going experience. And it is based on the false assumption that there are times in which you are not in direct contact with your nature. It creates the expectation that to be enlightened, to be free, one must perpetually have the same blissful, expanded experiences. Because all experiences come and go, this impossible expectation leads to repeated frustration and actually borders on nihilism.

The teaching that a veil can come between you and your nature, and that you peek through the veil at those times when you feel open confuses a particular feeling of openness with the openness from which feelings arise. You are always in direct contact with your nature as awareness. Enlightenment does not reside in a feeling; it is much vaster, sweeter and more effortless than this.

There is deep irony in this. In the satsang teachings, these oceanic states are usually not seen as experiences, since satsang is primarily interested in coarser and more tangible experiences such as emotions. But since they come and go, they are experiences. So when the satsang teaching fails to see these more subtle happenings as experiences, it privileges them by converting them into impossible experiential goals. This makes the goal just another phenomenal experience. A subtle one, but an experience all the same. What the nondual teachings speak about is more subtle and infinitely more pervasive than this.

Do you mean I am in contact with my nature even when I have doubts and confusion?

Yes. Doubts are simply passing objects, just like bubbles of bliss. They all come and go. Their arising and passing are directly noted by awareness – there is never a veil or covering.

You as awareness certify this at each moment.

Is there a way for me to be as sure of this as you seem to be?

Look very deeply. The Awareness that I'm speaking of isn't the activity of the brain. It is That to which appearances appear. Can you find a time when awareness is out of touch? When awareness is not present? Even in deep sleep, you are there as awareness, registering the fact that there are no objects at the time. Awareness is present – you are *presence* – in the midst of objects, in the absence of objects, and beyond all objects. Try to find a time when there is an object arising, pain, pleasure, bliss, anger, depression – when awareness is lacking.

Hmmm. So how does this mistake actually get made in satsang?

It often goes like this – it actually emerges in the teacher's performative cues as well as in the language. Let's try something, and I'll demonstrate what I mean.

OK.

So now close your eyes. (*speaking very slowly*) You may have questions or anxieties about your state. (*pause*) You may have yearnings to have a feeling of knowingness, a sense of security about yourself. Let these questions and yearnings arise in this very moment. (*pause*) Let them come up and be seen in the full light of your awareness. Don't solicit them, and don't chase them away. Rest in openness... (*pause, about half a minute goes by*)...

Mmmm…

Where are the questions and yearnings now?

There are not there.

That's it! Now open your eyes.

But I know the questions and yearning will come back.

Exactly, and what we just saw in our mini satsang emulation is just how the confusion arises. This very same procedure has been used in satsangs dozens of times. You attend the meeting with certain experiences you wish to transcend, including your doubts and questions. You are encouraged not to push these experiences away, but to open to them. A gentle frame of mind ensues, in which the undesirable experiences are not present. The teacher points to this moment by saying, "That's it!" or "You are there!" She may add that at this moment you are directly in touch with your true nature, without veils or coverings of any sort.

OK, so what's wrong with that?

Through the teacher's endorsement of this one moment, you are led to believe that the experience during this moment has a special, perhaps enlightened status. You end up chasing more moments like it, motivated by the impossible hope that they last forever. Because of the teacher's congratulatory remarks, you become dissatisfied with any other experiences.

But it wasn't an experience, it was a moment of direct seeing, wasn't it?

No more direct than barking your shin on the coffee table. It was a particular pleasant experience in which doubt wasn't present, but a feeling of spaciousness was. In satsang, the feeling of spaciousness tends to be misunderstood as the spaciousness which gives rise to all thoughts and feelings. So when the feeling of spaciousness is not present, you come to judge yourself as being out of touch with yourself. But you as pure spaciousness are never out of touch with anything. Passing feelings are just objects. You experienced the object of a phenomenal pleasantness which consisted of the lack of doubt and yearning. And the absence of one object is merely the presence of another object. Absences are a bit more subtle, so might not be treated as experiences in the same way as the emotional experiences favored in satsang. The very subtlety of the expanded feeling is responsible for its mis-characterization and the demand that it be present 100percent of the time.

I see now…

This misunderstanding is endemic to most of the satsangs I have seen or heard about. With teaching like this, the flip-flop is inevitable. No wonder you feel an intense desire to replicate those "That's it!" moments.

So what should the teacher do? How could he or she teach this kind of thing?

By *reducing* the felt distinction between moments, not *increasing* it.

How?

By piercing the myth of filtered access to your nature. This dualistic model is an introductory teaching metaphor, but at a certain point it was taken literally and became another piece of baggage. You can see through this myth by being true to your experience and checking for evidence of anything that blocks awareness. Can you find any such thing? And if you find something, consider this – its very ability to be "found" certifies it as not being apart from awareness. So just where is the block? Comfort is not the criterion of being in touch with awareness, and discomfort is not the criterion of being out of touch with awareness. On the contrary, *any* thought or feeling is brilliantly lit up by awareness, as awareness.

You will come to see that every moment is exactly like your "That's it!" moment.

You will find that you are always thoughtless just like in the satsang moments. This is because your nature is that space within which thought arises. Thought is free to arise, or not. And you are always in direct contact with awareness, because there is nowhere else to go, and nothing else available that can serve as a veil between you and awareness. There is never anywhere else for you to be. You are in unbroken contact with awareness because you *are* awareness. "You" and "awareness" – two words for the same thing.

And what is enlightenment?

The unshakeable knowledge that your nature as awareness has never included separation. Enlightenment is when the difference between enlightenment and unenlightenment drops away.

The Social Construction of Enlightenment

I must admit, when I think of being enlightened, I don't imagine myself at work on the midnight shift at the local 7-11!

That's a nice image from Steven Harrison. It points to the social construction of the "enlightenment" concept. Although there are traditional teachings with strict and specific definitions of the term, those traditions themselves are also social contexts. And for those people seeking enlightenment who don't see themselves as belonging to a traditional form of spirituality, "enlightenment" is quite a vague term. Its vagueness allows it to be filled in with whatever the heart desires, and most of the images have their social and cultural elements. The particular content of the images spring from whatever is considered desirable by the subculture where the term is employed.

Different traditions have their different models and personality profiles associated with enlightenment. These profiles carry images. In Zen the image is that you are stern, spontaneous, efficient and unpredictable. In Tibetan Buddhism you are kind, you laugh a lot and you become philosophical if the need arises. According to the Western satsang motif, your eyes are open and deep, you don't blink very much, you are mostly silent and if you speak it is very slowly. These images usually involve some form of being regarded by others.

This is why people don't usually imagine being enlightened yet residing in a cave or on a desert island. That would be too boring, and it doesn't contain any of the cultural desiderata that constitute the Enlightenment concept. No one imagines being enlightened in situations where other people are totally oblivious, treating you the same old way as before. You'd think, "What would be the point?"

Of course the teachings differ, but aren't they all talking about the same thing? Isn't true enlightenment the same everywhere?

You might feel like this is an essential place to begin. After all, no one wants to think that they are proceeding in the wrong direction. But as you proceed, you will find something curious happening. As your inquiry deepens, you will feel more and more free from the spell of images, including images of enlightenment. This reflects greater confidence, and less concern that you might have pursued a wrong path. You will enact fewer comparisons between self and others. You will be captivated by the warm, sweet calling of the search for the truth of yourself. It is what Jean Klein calls "higher reasoning." It doesn't take place through comparative images, but through a deep and intuitive opening towards perhaps a feeling of sweetness, or as a feeling of always having been home.

So as I get closer to enlightenment I will think less about enlightenment?

That's good! *(laughing)* The closer you get, the less it seems like a thing or destination or state or possession. The same can be said of every other "thing" as well!

This is also reflected in the various spiritual teachings too, if you look at them as a discourse. In a given book, website, or metaphysical tradition, you'll notice something happening as you progress through the material. The advertising portion of the teachings (the face they present to the public in the spiritual marketplace) relies more on the kinds of concrete enlightenment images we spoke about before. This is because these parts of the discourse also serve the purpose of getting you interested in the higher-level teachings. The more advanced the teachings, the less they paint pictures, and the more they concentrate on searching for the truth of things.

Increasing the Sense of Separation?

At certain times, you advise people to inquire deeply, or look into certain things. Doesn't this advice as advice merely strengthen the sense of personal doership? Isn't it less nondual when you advise people what to do?

The avoidance of recommendations is an idea from the teachings that used to be called "non-doership teachings" and which are now called "neo-advaita" teachings. I see spiritual advice as being on a par with what a physician or auto mechanic would tell you, and no spiritual teachings object to these conversations! So I don't think that advising someone to try something will cause the damage claimed by these teachings. In fact I think that advice will help in many cases.

Can you give an example?

First, let's see an example in which advice might *not* help. Some people feel a lot of guilt or anxiety from wanting to control or choose in just the right way. They might feel that their particular identity is closely tied up with being the agent of actions, and they feel the need to do the "right" things. They might be the people who say, "That's what I do, it's who I am." In these cases, hearing spiritual advice can increase their anxiety, as it only gives them more stuff to do, which they must perform correctly. In these cases, the anxiety can be reduced when they see the automaticity of actions they had thought they were responsible for. If actions are automatic events, then the whole notion of responsibility loses its stinging personal, judgmental, moral tone. The neo-advaitin descriptive teachings are a very effective and immediate antidote for issues like this. They hit the spot perfectly.

But there are many issues which aren't so explicitly tied up with choice and control. There are many people who don't feel that much investment in being a doer or controller. Their issue might be self-esteem, or they might feel identified with the body, or a set of memories. Prescriptive language can help in these cases.

Advice and recommendations don't exacerbate every issue the way they might exacerbate a feeling of controllership. In fact, the irony is that the neo-advaitin's carefully worded descriptive phrasing is lost on many students anyway. Many students just translate the teacher's descriptions right back into prescriptions for themselves. The teacher's "There's no one here" becomes the student's "If I keep attending these talks, then there will be no one here for me, either."

For example, in the direct path, one of the principal teachings is to take your stand as awareness. Once you know the truth even intellectually, you take your stand as that which you already know yourself to be. You don't need to wait for a transformation. Your subsequent experience will come to confirm the stand you have taken. Notice that this is a kind of doing, not just a case of hearing descriptions. And notice the irony that in spite of the neo-advaitin teacher's characterization of things, the student still sees himself as listening to the carefully crafted non-prescriptive descriptions. So he's *still* doing stuff!

But there really isn't a doer. So why speak as if there is?

(*laughs*) It seems like there's no doer. But does it seem that there really is a body or mind, or pencil or teacup? That's just the point. In the very same way that there's no doer, there's nothing else either. So why stop short? Sure, there's no separate controlling entity. If it's all awareness, then for the same reasons, there are no independent thoughts, feelings, actions, movements, objects, bodies or worlds. Speaking in terms of a doer isn't metaphysically different from speaking of a mind/body mechanism. If you say that one doesn't exist, then why does the other exist? Why stop right there? The same analysis applies to both, and to every supposedly objective thing. Inquiry will have stopped short, gaps will arise, separation will be felt, because the basis to which you used to attribute doership will be left in place.

For now, you can look at speaking in terms of a doer, like speaking of a sunset even though the sun doesn't actually settle down, or speaking of your car not "wanting" to start up even though your car doesn't have desires. In fact, *all* speaking is like this. Things don't exist "out there," independent of awareness. There is no borderline between "in" and "out." Things are merely awareness itself. This frees you from the responsibility to "accurately" capture things by speech, and yields the freedom to speak of everything.

A while ago, you said that advice is empty. Is this what you meant?

Good point! Yes, doership and the separate existence of a controlling entity aren't special metaphysically. Everything is empty of separate existence in this same way. All events of speaking, and all other things, are just like this.

The "Enlightenment" Story

Why don't you tell your enlightenment story in these conversations? After all, it's on your website.

Yes, such a story often tends to get the conversation going; but as the conversation proceeds, that story quickly melts away into what is always impersonally present everywhere. In this way, you could look at it as a bit of fragrance but not the rose itself. There are many other bits of fragrance as well.

There are several reasons I don't tell that story a lot. One is that stories like these can give the wrong impression about self-inquiry. They give the impression that the goal is a desirable personal state, such as a wonderful new set of feelings and experiences. Quite the opposite is the case. It is *not* personal. It is not home improvement. Rather, the goal is to know *that* in which the personal arises, that which is one's true nature. This knowing cannot be personal. As Jean Klein once quipped, "You can't see it; it's behind you."

Another reason I don't use that story very much is that "enlightenment" is a systematically vague term, especially outside traditional or detailed spiritual contexts. In traditional Shankaracharyan Advaita Vedanta or Madhyamika Buddhism, the terms are carefully defined, and people tend to agree on the vocabulary. But if you're not in a context like that, "enlightenment" is too vague to be useful. It functions like a placeholder for people's fondest wishes, hopes and dreams. For one person, enlightenment means getting over a hatred of their parents. For another, it might mean being able to travel internationally by levitation!

And then there's this. I find that when people hear these stories, their sense of separation is increased. They begin to divide people up into two classes, the "haves" and "have-not's." They feel left out. They look upon having such a story as the mark of success. The more they hear these stories, the more they desire to be among the "haves." Their spiritual search turns into a yearning to have a story of their own to tell.

Of course for a smaller group of people, it actually is helpful to hear stories like these. They want to speak to someone who presents himself as clearly having found what they themselves are seeking. This gets them going. So the story helps them choose a teacher, and the motivation helps internalize the teachings. But sooner or later they too will face the issue of attachment to these stories, to the expectation of gaining a new status or possession.

And what was your story?

(smiles) Do you perhaps fall into the latter group of people?

(laughs) *I guess so!*

It took me a long time before I knew there was such a thing as these stories. I didn't know how people reacted to them, that they were "an item," or sought after. I began to learn about this sometime later. One evening, I wrote an e-mail message about something that had happened years before when I was reading a book in the subway station. I hadn't mentioned it to anyone before. I didn't associate the word "enlightenment" with it. "Well, then, you're enlightened!" was the response. People came to regard it as "Greg's enlightenment experience." I didn't know what they were talking about until a few years later when I met more people involved in spiritual culture.

I also began to notice how people who didn't have a dramatic, transformational story to tell felt like they were missing something. They didn't consider themselves "done" until they too had a story. Often they tried to replicate the circumstances of their favorite stories, by traveling to the same place, or by trying to re-create the same set of circumstances they had heard about.

OK, so what was this story?

Ever since childhood I'd always been interested in finding out what or who I was. Who am I? What is the world? What is the difference? After living these questions for a long time, clarity came in two stages. The first stage could be characterized as the dissolution of the sense of separateness into effortless witnessing awareness. The second stage could be described as the peaceful collapse of this witness into pure awareness itself.

This first stage came about through my suspicion that

my nature depended on the willing, controlling, choosing function. Over the years I had seemingly eliminated every other possibility. I knew I couldn't be the body, the DNA, the brain cells, the mind, memories, values, or the waking, dreaming or deep sleep states. I felt that I was constant and featureless, observing these things as coming and going phenomena.

But I did have the sneaking suspicion that what made me Greg was the faculty of willing and choosing. I felt that if I could put my finger on this, it would be like revealing the Wizard of Oz behind the curtain.

So I began to try to accentuate this feeling, to bring it out into the open. I looked back through my life and asked myself, "When have I felt the most myself, the most like Greg?" The answer came that it was when I was deciding or choosing, especially those things that were out of the ordinary for me, such as my decision to take ballet lessons so I could audition for a job at Disneyland, or to join the Army, or go to graduate school, etc.

I set about trying to find the hidden place where this chooser resided. Shortly thereafter, I came upon Ramesh Balsekar's book, *Consciousness Speaks*. This was mid-1996, and here was a book that was all about the very issue of "doing" that I was already considering.

After a few months with this book, I was standing in Grand Central Station waiting for the subway to take me uptown. I was reading this one page of the book, and I saw in a flash that there can't be *any* choosing center. Choices and willing are just as unplanned and spontaneous as any other arising phenomenon. There cannot be a locatable center, here or anywhere else. All such "places" were seen as nothing more than arisings in awareness. The notion of people as separate centers of identity dissolved in a brilliant ball of light emanating from my chest area and expanding outward. Life became an effortless smooth flow, and the experience of myself or anyone being a separate center or independent individual has never returned.

The second stage was after this. There was no more individuated center or sense of choosing. There was no personal scorekeeping or interpersonal comparison. No sense of personhood in "myself" or attributed to any "one" else. There was no suffering or place for it to reside. There was, however, an ever so subtle sense of an offset – between this spacious awareness and the appearances that arose in awareness. This offset was experienced as a neutral but curious difference between subject and object. An example would be the difference between an arising sound and the awareness to which this sound appeared. The very experience of this arising, sweet as though it was, seemed as though it constituted an offset.

This offset didn't match the descriptions from the great texts I had read, such as the *Ashtavakra Gita*, the *Mandukya Upanishad*, and Nagarjuna's *Treatise on the Middle Way*. So I began to investigate what this offset could be.

I found that these great texts weren't much help when it came to what I considered to be the mechanics of this offset issue. No teacher's book of dialogs was any help either, because people just weren't asking about stuff like this. I wanted to know what accounted for the felt distinction when appearances were nothing other than awareness itself.

One day, a very subtle and sophisticated teacher tried to answer this question. He said that you can know that appearances are nothing other than awareness because they arise, subsist and subside into awareness. There can be, he said, nothing other for these appearances to be. But this was merely restating what was already my day-in and day-out experience. But I also had a strong feeling of kinship with the great texts, and a feeling of inspiration from them. I actually had an inviting feeling that this gap would soon dissolve. Yet this teacher's explanation seemed second-hand and inferential like "therefore it must be so." It didn't seem direct like "gapless awareness is my experience." I still felt this gap. And I thought that he probably did too.

Some time later, Francis Lucille told me he honored the teachings of Sri Atmananda and gave me a copy of *Atma Darshan*. When I read this small book, which is actually quite modern in spirit, I found that it put the finger on the issue of offset. Reading it and living with it, I experienced just the antidote to my impression of a gap between subject and object. Atmananda's exposition dissolved this distinction. This offset had no more room to be a separate "thing." It was no longer felt, it no longer made sense. Thanks to Francis's kindness and Atmananda's crystal-clear teachings, this sense of offset peacefully and joyously melted into the brilliant clarity of awareness, never to arise again.

Did you ever forget? Many people forget this and have to remember it again, myself included.

Not at all. It isn't the kind of thing that comes and goes. It isn't the kind of thing that is subject to forgetting or remembering. Sometimes psychologists call things like this a global shift in perception. It doesn't require rehearsal.

It's sort of like when I was 10 years old and I found out there was no Santa Claus. That Christmas Eve I had tiptoed downstairs about 3 a.m., in breathless anticipation of my Christmas gift. It was a bicycle that year. I saw my parents wrapping and labeling the presents. "Oh honey," said my mom to my dad, "Let's say that the bicycle is not from us but from Santa," as she wrote out the label. "Ah-ha!" I thought. "So *that's* how it is." And I never experienced Santa again in the same way. It became a polite community fiction. It wasn't something I ever had to remind myself. I never forgot. I've never fallen back into the belief that Santa Claus really does exist; I've never had to remind myself that he doesn't.

And you don't tell this story more because you think it won't help?

That's right. Some people are encouraged and inspired by these stories. It varies from person to person, but I've noticed that for many people, the more they hear stories like this, the more they want one for themselves. They see it as a kind of success story, and they focus on the story rather than the inquiry. They begin to feel that something like this must happen to them for their nature as awareness to be the case. Even a few teachers have confided in me that they feel somehow disqualified because of not having a story like this to tell. But events and narratives like this are themselves just arisings in awareness. The mind, body, world, the person – they are *all* arisings in awareness. No person has a story. A person *is* a story.

The ironic thing is that these stories seem significant only if one feels like there is a separate entity to begin with!

After someone no longer feels this sense of personal separation, then there's no need for a story about "me." There's a sense that all stories are about I as awareness, whether the narrative details are an Aesop's fable, an Arnold Toynbee's world history, or a Buddha's enlightenment story. There will be no place for envy or anxiety. There will be no preference for one story over another, and no feeling of being left out in the cold.

Attached to Awareness?

Many of your answers mention awareness and consciousness. Isn't that merely another view, and another attachment?

This is a very important question. There are other nondual teachings that don't make use of an all-embracing awareness notion. Some of my favorite nondual teachings are Pure Land Buddhism, Madhyamika Buddhism, and the recent Western nonessentialist, antifoundationalist teachings of Ludwig Wittgenstein, Jacques Derrida, Hans-George Gadamer, Richard Rorty, Stanley Fish, and others. And then there are the monotheistic paths such as mystical Christianity, Kabbala and Rosicrucianism.

In my private counseling work these different viewpoints may come up, depending on the background and inclinations of the person who's asking the questions.

But it's true, I do speak more from the awareness teachings such as Sri Atmananda's direct path – because they contain concepts and vocabulary that most people are already comfortable with.

But then which teachings are true*?*

That's just the point. To think one of these teachings is a true or accurate depiction of the world, and to think the other teachings are not true – that's just what it means to be attached to a teaching. It still depends on a felt dualism between appearance and reality.

When one's seeking takes one to an inquiry about reality, there is a yearning for a teaching that tells you the accurate truth about the world. But the deeper they get in their inquiry, the more they come to see that it makes no sense to compare the degree of "accuracy" of these various teachings. And why? Comparing theories of the world to the world itself is not like comparing photos of the Eiffel Tower to the Eiffel Tower. You can't look at the world without being embedded in some kind of theory-bound element. Even the ordinary "I'm in here – the world's out there" notion is the popular science of 200 years ago serving as our everyday intuitions today. To compare worldviews for accuracy the way you compare photos would require you to step out of your skin, as it were. The very tool you would use to compare views is itself another view. No one has ever done this and it is incoherent to try.

But there's hope! There is no need to find a separate place or a world beyond views, for *that* which is free of views is not a place. It is not a separately defined location or vantage point. It is not a state of omniscience. It is that clarity from which views, locations and states arise, and it is available as your experience at this very moment. The very fact that you see is evidence that seeing is known and embraced by this awareness, which is your nature.

You do not need to reconcile these teachings with each other. Leave that to the professors of comparative philosophy.

It's perhaps more helpful to see these teachings as expedient means to the end of suffering. Think of them as tools rather than pictures.

I see how one can be attached to a certain teaching, like the aware-ness teachings. But within that teaching, can you be attached to awareness itself?

Yes, you can. In fact, the seasoned awareness teachings such as traditional Advaita Vedanta and the direct-path teach-ings actually anticipate this attachment, and make use of it in the teachings themselves. In fact, if the student doesn't attach to the concepts, the teaching probably isn't making a deep enough impression to be transformational. The Dalai Lama once said about the Buddhist emptiness teachings that if they don't make you feel like your life is being turned upside down, then you're not taking them to heart closely enough. And as the teachings proceed, the student's attach-ment dissolves at that certain level, and shifts "upward" to become attached at a more subtle level. This is actually how the teachings proceed. This movement or dynamic is quite purposeful, and is called "sublation."

Sublation, can you explain that a bit more?

In these teachings, sublation happens when you have an experiential flash of insight that dissolves a certain under-standing you had. You thought things were a certain way. But then see through the presuppositions of this older understanding by coming to understand a more subtle and more thorough teaching. This new understanding not only accounts for what you had thought before, but it also carries you further. The previous understanding was sublated or undercut by the new understanding.

Ah! It sounds very intense and experiential. Can you give me an example?

Sure. Many different paths, especially the older paths, proceed like this. They had lots of time to see what things were able to undercut other things.

For example, in formal Advaita Vedanta, there are three levels of teaching on the creation of the world. Each model is simpler to understand, and yet more dualistic, than the one which follows. Each one is taught to show how Brahman or absolute consciousness is continuous with and non-different from the world, and to reduce the student's felt distinctions between self and other, self and world, self and Brahman.

The first one taught is *Srishti-Drishti Vada* (pronounced "shrishtee-DRISHtee vada"), which holds that the creation of the world precedes perception of the world. The student assumes the reality of the world, so they are taught that Brahman created the world. And one effect of this creation is that we perceive this world. Sooner or later the student comes to question the presuppositions of this explanation.

At this point in the formal teachings, the student may be told, "OK, here's what *really* happens," and they'll be given the next model, *drishti-srishti vada* (pronounced "drishtee-SHRISHtee vada"), which holds that cognition and creation are simultaneous. Not that cognition causes creation, but that they arise simultaneously. This serves to sublate the notion of a causal relation between the world and experience, while diminishing the force of a feeling of multiple souls experiencing the world. And with continued teachings, sooner or later the student might come to question the very notion that self and world are different.

At this point the student may be given the final model in this series, *ajati vada* (no creation ever happened). This is of course more difficult to understand, but it helps diminish the feeling of a difference between self and world.

OK, but why not give them the real truth right away?

OK. "You and the world are nothing but awareness." How's that?

I hear it, but I don't really feel it or understand it.

And that's exactly why some paths use smaller, more comprehensible steps. You can make each step yours by really experiencing its truth, not just in a verbal or intellectual way. And at each level sooner or later, you will come to question certain things in the teaching you were given. This is the point at which this level begins to destabilize and become sublated. And you grasp the teaching whose insights sublated it. And so on...

I see. And does this ever end? Is there a final sublation?

Yes. In the direct path teachings, the ones we are speaking about now, the last sublation is the point at which all dualities have dissolved. You could say at this point that awareness shines in its own glory.

And so how do you keep from becoming attached to awareness? Is that concept ever sublated?

Good question! The notion of everything being awareness is an attachment only when it is maintained by force of hope or belief. But after it becomes your experience, then the belief will no longer be needed. Things will no longer need to appear as awareness, and the concept will gently sublate itself, doing so with, you might say, a good sense of humor.

This happens in a sweet and automatic way. Take the example of Atmananda's direct-path teachings. Awareness is a teaching tool used to capture intuitions you already have. It also serves as a way to deconstruct your notion that things other than awareness truly exist. You tend to think of existing things as being the same kind of object that you take yourself to be.

That is, what you take yourself to be determines what you feel the world to be made of. If you think you are a body, then you see the world as made up of other physical objects existing apart from your body. If you think you are a subtle essence such as the mind, then you will see the world as made up of subtle essences and energies existing separately from your mind. If you see yourself as awareness, you will see the world also as being nothing other than awareness.

But then an amazing thing happens. When you no longer really think of yourself as a physical or subtle object, then you won't carry the belief that you are awareness either. This belief will sweetly evaporate, having become unnecessary. It will no longer be necessary, having done its work. For the very notion of awareness gets it meaning in contradistinction to things other than awareness. Mountains and rivers become mountains and rivers again. When either side of the distinction is seen through, the distinction itself dissolves. And with it, any possibility of attachment. This is your freedom.

Index

NON-DUALITY PRESS

If you enjoyed this book, you might be interested in these related titles published by Non-Duality Press.

CONSCIOUS.TV

Conscious.tv is a TV channel broadcasting on the Internet at www.conscious.tv. Certain programmes are also broadcast on Satellite TV stations based in the UK. The channel aims to stimulate debate, question, enquire, inform, enlighten, encourage and inspire people in the areas of Consciousness, Healing and Psychology.

There are already over 100 interviews to watch including several with communicators on Non-Duality including Gangaji, Jeff Foster, Catherine Noyce, Richard Lang, Roger Linden, Tony Parsons, Genpo Roshi, Richard Sylvester, Rupert Spira, Florian Schlosser and Francis Lucille. Some of these interviewees also have books available from Non-Duality Press.

Do check out the channel as we are interested in your feedback and any ideas you may have for future programmes. Email us at info@conscious.tv with your ideas or if you would like to be on our newsletter list.

WWW.CONSCIOUS.TV

CONSCIOUS.TV and *NON-DUALITY PRESS*
present two unique DVD releases

CONVERSATIONS ON NON-DUALITY – VOLUME 1
Tony Parsons – *The Open Secret* • Rupert Spira –
The Transparency of Things – Parts 1 & 2 • Richard Lang –
Seeing Who You Really Are

CONVERSATIONS ON NON-DUALITY – VOLUME 2
Jeff Foster – *Life Without a Centre* • Richard Sylvester –
I Hope You Die Soon • Roger Linden – *The Elusive Obvious*

Available to order from: www.non-dualitypress.com

LaVergne, TN USA
20 November 2010
205712LV00003B/90/P